W9-CRU-874

SHARE THE WORD NOW

Share the Word Now

ALBERT McCLELLAN

BROADMAN PRESS
NASHVILLE, TENNESSEE

© Copyright 1973 · Broadman Press
All rights reserved
4284–15
0–8054–8415–9

Library of Congress Catalog Card Number: 72–94402
Dewey Decimal Classification: 248.5
Printed in the United States of America

Contents

1] [Renewal of the Word

A young man walked out of a Sunday School class after hearing the story of Daniel in the lions' den and said, "Same old stuff that I've heard all my life." Well, perhaps it was for him the "same old stuff" if his teacher was too dull to relate it to modern times. It did not need to be "the same old stuff," for Daniel's story speaks to lonely moral man in the midst of the great social and personal terrors of our times. This young man no doubt had heard only the clichés, not the truth. He was told a story, not brought face to face with its reality. He felt aversion, not challenge.

Things do not need to be this way, and if the churches are to live victoriously, they must not be this way. We must see the Bible with fresh eyes, searching its ideas for truth relevant to our own day. We must teach the Bible as intimately related to the disturbing problems of life. We must see it as responsive to every modern human need.

The real tragedy for that young man was that he had more personal problems than he could count; yet the teacher missed all of them. He was like many young people who wait longingly for the kind of help the Bible can give to them. They may not know they wait, but they wait, trying all of the world's empty panaceas, such as astrology, mysticism, magic, science, art, drugs—some good, some bad; yet none of them healing.

Only God can heal, but he does not heal apart from his truth that comes as new light out of the pages of the Bible. "For the word of God is quick, and powerful, and sharper than any twoedged sword, piercing even to the dividing asunder of soul and spirit, and of the joints and marrow, and is a discerner of the thoughts and intents of the heart" (Heb. 4:12).

A Christian layman who travels forty states in his work said: "I've listened to many preachers and teachers of the Bible. Some present the Bible as if a great wall is fixed between now and then, its truth holding no relevancy to the present day, and with no handles for the modern man. Others present it as a kind of a vapid latter-day morality with no integrity and no authority. One is too *other* worldly, the other is too *this* worldly, and both fail to reach me in my basic moral and spiritual needs. It is the truly inspiring preacher or teacher who breaks through the wall and ties the past and the present together." If one man loyal to Christ feels this way, how must other men feel who have no loyalty to him?

There can be no lasting church renewal without biblical renewal. God himself is waiting to pour out blessings upon this world as men become awakened to the Bible's direct bearing on all of their contemporary problems.

He speaks through his Word that we might see his Son Jesus Christ whom he has also called the Word. "In the beginning was the Word, and the Word was with God, and the Word was God. The same was in the beginning with God. All things were made by him; and without him was not anything made that was made" (John 1:1–3). The Scriptures and Jesus Christ are inseparably bound together, a union for the communication of God's love to man. Jesus in his great prayer to the Father said, "I have given unto them the words which thou gavest me; and they have received them, and have known surely that I came out from thee, and they have believed that thou didst send me. . . . Sanctify them through thy truth: thy word is truth" (John 17:8,17).

God comes boldly and graciously to man through Christ, his personal Word and the Bible, his written Word. The renewal of the written Word in our midst can lead to the renewal of the personal Word, and through them God will speak to us. John Calvin, the great French reformer, said that through the Scriptures God opens "his own holy mouth." One could add that in Jesus Christ God opens his own holy heart. Jesus said, "He that heareth my word, and believeth on him that sent me, hath everlasting life" (John 5:24) and "Search the scriptures, for in them ye think ye have eternal life: and they are they which testify of me" (John 5:39).

The word becomes the Word and truth becomes Truth and life becomes Life. Wherever the personal Word is renewed in human experience, it is because the written Word has been renewed, for indeed through the Scriptures God opens "his own holy mouth" to show us his own holy heart. God speaks through the Bible out of the past to the present.

God's Voice Out of the Past

"The Bible is a musty old book" is the way some people see the Word of God. "Myths" and "fairy tales" are the ways others see it. Many people do not see it at all, or else they make it a book of magic or a badge of respectability. They do not have the faintest idea of the great events written on its pages or the power that it has for the transformation of life. If they read it, they are appalled at how ancient and remote it sounds, and they dismiss it as belonging to the dead past.

The Bible does indeed belong to the past, but this does not mean that it is of no importance for the present. It is ancient but it is vital, for in its pages God reveals himself at work in human history and in human personality. Time is not a restriction to God, and the fact that he spoke to man as early as he did does not mean that he immediately left man and has no more to say to him. It is God's way to point to the past as he speaks in the present. He appeared to Jacob as the God of Abraham, and to David as the God of Jacob. Jesus on the mount of transfiguration talked with Moses and Elijah of the past and to the disciples of the present. The past in the Bible speaks to the present.

The Bible Is the Wisdom of the Ages

It is not only God's wisdom but man's wisdom too as man stumbles through history in darkness toward the light. Moses reminded the Jews that the statutes of God "is your wisdom and your understanding in the sight of the nations" (Deut. 4:6), and in the Chronicles it is written as "the word which he commanded to a thousand generations" (1 Chron. 16:15).

In a small Texas town the most prominent atheist was also a lawyer. People could never understand why he always used examples from the Bible in his jury trials. Some people believed it was because most of the jurors were Christians and familiar with the Bible. Toward the end of his life the lawyer became a Christian himself and said, "From my childhood I have been drawn to the Bible as a book of great wisdom. All my life I have been guided by its Proverbs."

This simple testimony by one whose life had been finally conquered by what the Scriptures once said proved what David said long ago: "The law of the Lord is perfect, converting the soul; the testimony of the Lord is sure, making wise the simple" (Ps. 19:7).

In 1864 some members of a black congregation presented a Bible to Abraham Lincoln. He said in response, "This great book . . . is the best gift God has given to man . . . but for it we could not know right from wrong."

There is a sense in which the Bible is a holy partnership between God's perfection and man's imperfection. In its pages we see the greatness and glory of God reaching down to man who responds in heroic but sometimes stumbling attempts to escape his sin and his littleness. We hear God speaking through Christ the lofty words of acceptance "Suffer little children, and forbid them not, to come unto me; for of such is the kingdom of heaven" (Matt. 19:14). We also hear the revengeful Israelites singing, "Happy shall be he that taketh and dasheth thy little ones against the stones" (Ps. 137:9). These two sayings do not make the Bible inconsistent and false, but rather prove it to be both an immensely human and an immensely divine book. Only Christ is sinless; not human beings, whether they live in Bible times or in modern times.

God in his wisdom made the Bible a very wise book by selecting writers of different gifts and temperaments and directing them to write against the backgrounds of the cultural and historical viewpoints of their own times. In other words, God let man put himself into the Bible, sometimes his worst self, sometimes his best self. The result is an authentic autograph of God and man in dialogue, a believable book that has never disappointed any who have given their lives to it.

The glory of the Bible's wisdom and truth is like the pulsars in outer space, one of which is only about twelve miles in diameter and yet has a mass almost the same as the sun. The pulsars are collections of squeezed matter, composed only of the nuclei of atoms. One cubic inch weighs five million tons. As the pulsars turn, they emit radio signals and light flashes, which men on earth hear and see. The Bible is a book of fire and light; it is compacted truth and fully capable of exploding into a spiritual solar system all its own. The Bible is indeed wisdom of the ages.

Probably the poorest approach to the Bible is to think of it as literature, as perhaps like Chaucer but different in language, or like Goethe but different in structure, or like Shakespeare but different in purpose. Many of the college literary courses in the Bible are empty and ineffective and soon lose their appeal and their students. To come to the Bible as if it were only another book is a futile and frustrating experience. It must be approached with awe and a sense of surrender to its message, if one is to gain from it a satisfying and lasting experience. It will not open itself to doubters and critics.

The proof of the Scriptures is what they do inside the human heart. Jesus said, "God is love," and out of this grew the community of love; Paul said, "Pray without ceasing," and for two thousand years prayer rises from the churches; Peter said, "Humble yourselves under the mighty hand of God," and a great procession of worshipers bow their knees through the centuries unto this present hour. The truths of the Bible are the nuclei of the kingdom of God, and like faith, they are the substance of things unseen. The Bible's proof is its results in changed lives.

Why is there so much more to the Bible than its mere words?

1. The purpose of God lies at the heart of it. The psalmist prayed, "For ever, O Lord, thy word is settled in heaven" (Ps. 119:89). Jesus said, "Heaven and earth shall pass away: but my words shall not pass away" (Mark 13:31). Take away from the world the knowledge of God found in the Bible, and it would be an empty, hopeless, senseless, and constantly retrogressing place of cruel existence. In this world of strange values, even the most flagrant atheist lives by the theological hope given by the Bible.

2. The power of God is deep within the Bible. Power and truth belong together. Jesus said, "Ye do err, not knowing the scriptures, nor the power of God" (Matt. 22:29). Paul drew a terrible picture of the word of God: "the sword of the Spirit" (Eph. 6:17). The writer of the Hebrews said it was a "two-edged sword, piercing to the division of soul and spirit, of joints and marrow, and discerning the thoughts and intentions of the heart" (Heb. 4:12, RSV).

3. The Bible speaks to the deepest longings of the human soul. There is not a sigh it cannot answer, or a hunger it cannot fill; there

is not a heart it cannot comfort, or restless spirit it cannot still. The tired and weary cry out for solace, and it answers, "Come unto me, all ye that labour" (Matt. 11:28). The sick and imprisoned lift their somber songs and it replies, "I am the way, the truth, and the life" (John 14:6). William Cowper says: "A glory guilds the sacred page, majestic like the sun; it gives a light to every age; it gives, but borrows none." David said, "Thy word is a lamp unto my feet, and a light unto my path" (Ps. 119:105).

4. The Holy Spirit is the power through which its truth is opened. People who read the Bible without awareness of the need for special help from God to understand will never know the depths and the riches of the Bible. Indeed Paul saw it as the tool by which God's Spirit does his work, calling the Word of God "the sword of the Spirit" (Eph. 6:17). The Bible comes to us as a movement of the Holy Spirit. "No prophecy ever came by the impulse of man, but men moved by the Holy Spirit spoke from God" (2 Pet. 1:21, RSV). Its gospel comes to us "not only in word, but also in power and in the Holy Ghost" (1 Thess. 1:5).

The same power that pulsates the pulsars and creates new galaxies of solar systems pulsates the Bible and explodes its truth into millions of hearts, and through this exploding truth God is always reentering human history and altering human destiny.

An Imperishable Monument to God's Presence in History

The Bible is confrontation between God and man: God speaks, man answers; man speaks, God answers. This takes place mostly through the great transactions of history, such as Abraham's flight from Ur, the Exodus of God's people from Egypt, the Babylonian captivity of the Israelites and the birth, life, and advent of Christ. The majesty of these transactions is to be seen in what was disclosed, as William Temple put it, "not truth concerning God, but the living God Himself." These transactions are the doors of God entering into history; and the Bible is the graphic, profound description of the doors.

God guides these events with unerring hands. He gives his voice to his prophets to interpret them, and he opens the ears of the people to hear them and their minds to understand them. He opens their hearts to see him in the midst of these mighty events. Some events are more important than others. It was a great day, for example, when Moses led the Israelites out of Egypt, but it was a far greater day when Christ was born and "the Word was made flesh" (John 1:14).

The Bible view of God in history is unique in the world's religious literature, and the marvel of it is, that the Bible holds God present and at work in all of history. The more one reads the Bible, the more one realizes this is true. The agnostic may say, "The truth of the Bible depends on the view of him who reads it." He says this in criticism, yet what he says is true. The agnostic approaches the Bible with doubt and finds it untrue; the believer approaches it with faith and finds it true. If an agnostic history teacher says God is not in history, one should not be surprised, for as God said in another connection, "He that cometh to God must believe that he is" (Heb. 11:6). The key to finding God in history, as well as to finding him in one's own life is to approach the Bible with a sense of openness and humility. After all, the real discovery is not words about God, but God himself. It is the confrontation of persons, not ideas, and requires the same kind of understanding that exists where one person establishes communion with another person.

More than the Communication of Ideas

When God gave man the Ten Commandments, he did not send them floating on wings out of the sky, but he entered into conversation with a man named Moses on the top of Mount Sinai. In the Bible God is shown as trying to reach men through other men. His messengers were often far from perfect, like David who could write out of his most prayerful soul the twenty-thrid Psalm and yet out of his hottest anger, a prayer for revenge; or like Elijah who one day was a great prophet warning Ahab and Jezebel and the next day, a miserable coward skulking in the wilderness. The thing to look for in these messengers is not perfection in character or consistency even in what they said and did, but to the unerring finger of God as it points through them throughout the ages to Jesus Christ.

The Bible is the story of God moving toward man in Jesus Christ, reaching out for man and saving man. It is the spiritual dialogue of God and man, the face-to-face meeting of God and man in Jesus Christ. The Bible has just one purpose, to bring men to the knowledge of Jesus Christ. He is the Word of God for which the Word was written. John said it clearly at the end of his Gospel, "Many other signs truly did Jesus in the presence of his disciples which are not written in this book: but these are written that ye might believe that Jesus is the Christ, the Son of God; and that believing ye might have life through his name" (John 20:30–31).

Unless one goes beyond its letters to find its spirit, one has not discovered the Bible at all. Grappling mentally with Paul's great passages on predestination is one thing, but meeting Christ face-to-face in them is another. Important as Bible ideas are, it is the meeting that is really important. This is the reason that the Bible should always be approached as experience, for surely unless one does experience its depths in Christ, he has not read it at all. As an ancient book, the Bible is God's voice speaking out of the past, yet as experience it is God's voice in the present.

God's Voice in the Present

The Bible is the book the world cannot forget. For nearly two thousand years it has endured every kind of private and public attack, and yet it lives, more alive than ever. In modern times the Communists have tried to eradicate it from Russian life, burning it and jailing its preachers. As a gesture of denial, they sold one of the oldest and rarest manuscripts of the New Testament to the British Museum. They closed the seminaries and the churches and outlawed church schools, but still the Bible stands in Russia, very much alive, and even quoted by statesmen. In China, where once it was widely honored, the sayings of Mao have appeared to take its place. There too the schools of the Bible have been destroyed and the believers of the Bible tortured. There has been a frenzied attack on all Christians as if they were the blame for all of China's ills. Yet it lives with Christians reported to be memorizing entire books so as to keep it alive in their hearts.

Even in America, novelists and playrights have ignored the Bible, poets have derided it and critics maligned it, but strangely it has emerged again as the most printed and widely read book in our land. One version alone, the new *Today's English Version* of the American Bible Society has printed more than 35,000,000 copies since its first appearance in 1966.

Why does the Bible continue to live? For the simple reason that people have found that God speaks to them out of its pages even in these sophisticated and cynical times. They believe that its insights and revelations are as appropriate for present human experience as they were for ancient human experience. Unbelievers cannot accept this; to them the words of the Bible are lifeless and full of error. This is because they do not have the Holy Spirit to illumine their minds and to convince them that out of its depths God speaks to the heart of man in every life circumstance.

Speaks Only to Those Who Come to It by Faith

We know that God in the hearts of man was the original author of Scripture. Do we also know that he is its continuing author, and that he perpetually speaks from the Bible to the believers to bring new and unfolding meaning from it? Do we recognize that through Scripture there is a living transaction taking place between the God who is and the people who believe in him? Paul wrote to Timothy that "all scripture is inspired by God" (2 Tim. 3:16, RSV). The word "inspired" may also be interpreted as "breathed." Scripture then is "God breathed." Those who live by faith, finding their sustenance from the truth of the Word of God, are those who live by the breath of God.

The reason so many people fail to get anything from the Bible is that they refuse to give themselves to it. One young man vehemently assails the Bible as empty and meaningless, and as the reason for so many closed minds in today's society. Curiously in the name of freedom and openness he refuses to open its pages. He is disturbed in seeing people go to church with the Bible in their hands, and when someone presses a Bible verse upon him, he becomes angry and resentful. This young man who claims so much freedom and openness is actually a miserably closed person. He is afraid of the power of the Scriptures and refuses to give himself to them, lest he lose his independence. He does not know that he cannot even know about the Bible with a closed mind.

Faith is the surrender of ourselves to something in order to know its full reality. When Jesus said, "I am come that they might have life, and that they might have it more abundantly" (John 10:10), he was describing both his mission and his gift. He was also describing one of the outcomes of faith, for whoever believes in him will find his mind and heart abundantly strengthened. Surrendering to Jesus Christ, we know his reality; surrendering to his Word, we know its reality.

God speaks to people who approach the Bible with faith. Even though its language is different from the mod language of today and its customs rooted in ancient rural life, it responds to the open and devout heart as no other book in the world. The reason, of course, is that it is a living book, and God continues to inspire its readers and its scholars just as long ago he inspired its writers—both through the miracle of faith.

An Immensely Alive Book for Those Who Accept It

We must face it, a great many people have written the Bible off, denying its credibility, its authority, and its relevance, having arrived at this position on hearsay. They have rejected it not from knowledge, but from ignorance. They have heard well-meaning believers make claims for the Bible that did not agree with their experience, and so they have cried out, "fairy tales."

What are some of these claims that turn people off?

First, that it is a book of science. The Bible nowhere makes that claim for itself. Those who think about it like this have a difficult time explaining such things as an earth with four corners (Ezek. 7:2), a heaven held up with pillars (Job 26:11), and a sea above the sky (Ps. 148:4).

Second, that it is a book of history. Surely the Bible contains history, a great deal of it, but it also has allegory, poetry, and philosophy. The history it does contain is to a very special point, the knowledge of God through Jesus Christ. To make it a history of the Jews, doing what Josephus does in his great book, is to miss the meaning of the Bible, for it most certainly is not a detailed saga of the Hebrew people; rather it is an account of God's dealings with men through the Jews, the summing up of God's entry into human experience.

Third, that all Scripture has equal meaning and authority. Jesus himself said, "It hath been said . . . but I say unto you" (Matt. 5:31–32). To classify a profound passage like Romans 8 on salvation or 1 Corinthians 13 on love with sayings of Solomon or the story of Abraham's slaughter of the kings does not make sense, anymore than

16

equating Paul's glorious affirmation of the resurrection in 1 Corinthians 15 with the despondent preacher's denial of immortality in Ecclesiastes 9:4–6. This is not to say that the Bible is a contradiction of itself or that any of it is uninspired. Instead, all Scripture is the light in which any isolated passage is to be understood. Some of it is God's revelation of the inconsistencies and sinfulness of man, and of man's misunderstanding of God, while some of it is God's revelation of himself.

If we would have other people accept the Bible for what it truly is, and to live by it as a lamp unto their feet, we must show them that it is a book of God's dealings with man, his way of reaching out for man and offering him the knowledge of his love and of his Son.

We must also show them that it is a book of meaning for contemporary human experience, and a book of faith for their tired hearts. We must show them that as Emil Bruner has said, it is a kind of a sentence, the Old Testament being the first half and the New Testament, the second half, each half requiring the other half, and both required for the meaning of the whole. We must show them that it is indeed a sentence that says, "God shows his love for us in that while we were yet sinners Christ died for us" (Rom. 5:8, RSV).

Holds Strange Power to Make or Break Life

The Bible can make life, we have all believed, but can it break life too? To answer this question, look at what Jesus said at the end of his Sermon on the Mount. "Every one then who hears these words of mine and does them will be like a wise man who built his house upon the rock; and the rain fell, and the floods came, and the winds blew and beat upon that house, but it did not fall, because it had been founded on the rock. And every one who hears these words of mine and does not do them will be like a foolish man who built his house upon the sand; and the rain fell, and the floods came, and the winds blew and beat against that house, and it fell; and great was the fall of it" (Matt. 7:24–27, RSV).

But when Jesus said "my words" was he really talking about the Bible? Perhaps, not as a book, for the complete Bible was not then in existence. He was talking about his teachings that later were recorded in the Bible, and no doubt he was talking too about his teachings in the larger context of all the words and wisdom of God. The point is so simple that multitudes miss it: to ignore the wisdom of God in the making of one's own life is to build one's life on the sand. There is tragedy ahead on the road of life for all who ignore the wisdom of the Bible.

In the end, if a whole view of the Bible is taken, it is impossible for one to separate Jesus Christ and the words of God. In some ways, the personal Word and the written Word are one; at least they merge together as God's great loving reach for man. Peter wrote of Christ the "living stone, rejected by men but in God's sight chosen and precious" (1 Pet. 2:4, RSV). He drew a picture of men building a house out of stone, but discarding one stone that should have been used as the foundation.

Since this stone is left on the ground, the builders themselves stumble over it and are destroyed. The stone that should have become the cornerstone of their house actually becomes the stone of their destruction. Peter then concludes, " 'A stone that will make men stumble, a rock that will make them fall'; for they stumble because they disobey the word, as they were destined to do" (1 Pet. 2:8, RSV). The word does not break the man; rather he breaks himself against it. Scott wrote,

> Within that awful volume lies
> The mystery of mysteries!
> Happiest they of human race,
> To whom God has granted grace
> To read, to fear, to hope, to pray,
> To lift the latch and force the way;
> And better had they ne'er been born
> Who reads to doubt, or reads to scorn.

Belongs Both to Me and to All of God's People

Matthew Henry once said the Scriptures were "Shallows where a lamb could wade and depths where an elephant would drown." He was thinking the simplicity and the profundity of the Bible. On the one hand the most uneducated laborer can read and understand its pages; on the other hand the most educated scholar can find in its words a depth that will challenge a lifetime of study.

This axis of the simple and the profound can be seen in the lives of my two grandfathers who were born in the 1850's. One was the son of a simple farmer who lost his life in the Civil War. The boy was reared without any education, not even one year of schooling. He married without knowing how to read and write. But soon afterward he was converted, and my grandmother began to read to him from the Bible. He was so interested that he learned from the Bible to read the Bible, and became a lifelong student and teacher of its mysteries.

My other grandfather was the son of a newspaper editor and learned to read while working in his father's print shop, even before he went to school. A bright child, he learned Latin and Greek and attended university, rare for youth in those days. He was ordained a preacher and spent his long life teaching the Bible from a scholar's viewpoint.

In both cases, the Bible belonged to these men as something precious, a rare personal possession to be treasured and guarded. Each held a different view of the Bible, one being a Baptist, the other a Presbyterian, yet as neighbors they were friends. Their special interpretations of the Bible did not mean they would deny other people the right to their interpretations. Both men were willing to accept for study the views of others. In the years I knew these old men, I saw them grow in their understanding of the Scriptures because they were willing to examine the insights of others.

Truly, the Bible belonged to them. It was their personal book, a light and a lamp to show them their ways. They interpreted it for themselves, yet they did not arrive at their interpretations without advice from others. They did not cling to their own traditions *above* the Word of God, nor did they cling to their own traditions *about* the Word of God. They were both willing to let the Bible speak to them out of the experiences of all men.

Their approach to the Bible was fashioned by Peter's great words, "We have also a more sure word of prophecy; whereunto ye do well that ye take heed, as unto a light that shineth in a dark place, until the day dawn, and the day star ariseth in your hearts; knowing this first, that no prophecy of the scripture is of any private interpretation. For the prophecy came not in old time by the will of man: but holy men of God spake as they were moved by the Holy Ghost" (2 Pet. 1:19).

These two men were the children of the Reformation, one going back through his family to the stormy days of John Knox in Scotland, and the other through his family to the cradling of the Anabaptist movement in Holland. Both were intensely individualistic, and shaped by the forces of the Reformation, a basic point of which was the right to read and decide on the meaning of the Scriptures for oneself; yet both knew still that the true greatness of the Bible is that it belongs to all men.

Must Be Shared to Be Possessed

Scott said the Bible was an "awful volume" containing "the mystery of mysteries." By "awful" he did not mean "bad" but "awe inspiring." It is a book to be looked at with wonder. Not only does it contain a "mystery of mysteries"; it is "a mystery of mysteries," not as merely another mystery among a world of mysteries, but as a profound mystery filled with other mysteries. One of these mysteries is that it is a living book which lives for those who possess it as they hold out its truths to others.

There are three attitudes possible toward the Bible (a) taking it *superstitiously* as a good luck charm, (b) taking it as *meaningless* and as a drag on the world or (c) taking it *seriously* as a book to be studied and shared. Those who take it as superstition are little more moved by it than those who take it as meaningless. For them it is a dead book, musty and stale, empty and vague, unreal and unappealing. Those who take it seriously find that it is a living book, becoming more and more alive as they read it and share it.

The more we talk to others about the Bible and its truth, the more precious it becomes to us. This is the reason a Sunday School where the Bible is really studied is always a growing dynamic fellowship. It is only when people talk about other things, or when their knowledge of the Bible becomes secondhanded that Sunday Schools fail and churches decline. The study of the Bible is God's open door to the human heart. The disciples who walked with Jesus on the way to Emmaus and talked with him about the Scriptures later said, "Did not our heart burn within us . . . while he opened to us the scriptures?" (Luke 24:32).

Our task then is to share the Word, for in sharing the Word, we testify of Jesus Christ. In sharing the Word, we hold out to man the wonderful words of life. When Moses gave God's law to his people, the transmission of that law was through words, God's words. They were to be more than words on a tablet of stone. The urgency can be seen in one of the great passages of the Old Testament, "These words you must learn by heart, this charge of mine; you must impress them on your children, you must talk about them when you are sitting at home and when you are on the road, when you lie down and when you rise up. You must tie them on your hand as a momento, and wear them on your forehead as a badge; you must inscribe them on the door-posts of your houses and on your gates" (Deut. 6:6–9, Moffatt).

Share the Word now! This is God's call to us while it is yet day, for night is surely coming when there can be no sharing. Indeed, the night is already here for many, for they have hardened their hearts, to the point of having eyes and seeing not and ears and hearing not.

Share the Word now! God's mighty injunction is upon us. He has spoken clearly, "O earth, earth, earth hear the word of the Lord" (Jer. 22:29). "Hear ye, and give ear; be not proud: for the Lord hath spoken" (Jer. 13:15). "Seek ye out of the book of the Lord, and read: no one of these shall fail" (Isa. 34:16). "Give ear, O my people, to my law: incline your ears to the words of my mouth" (Ps. 78:1).

Share the Word now! "Preach the word; keep at it in season and out of season, refuting, checking, and exhorting men; never lose patience with them; and never give up your teaching; for the time will come when people will decline to be taught sound doctrine, they will accumulate teachers to suit themselves and tickle their own fancies, they will give up listening to the Truth and turn to myths" (2 Tim. 4:2–5, Moffatt).

Share the Word now! For to share it is to preach Christ.

O Word of God incarnate
   O Wisdom from on high
O truth unchanged, unchanging
   O light of our dark sky.

2] [Church Renewal
Through the Word

Styles in words change. We can see this by the way such words as "parlour," "living room," "den," "family room" and "Florida room" have been used in different times and places to mean the same thing. Yet as time goes on, the meanings sharpen, becoming precise and definitive. "Parlòr" is a more or less formal "living room." "Den" is a retreat-type room. "Family room" is a kind of an informal or secondary "living room." A "Florida room" is a family room in Florida.

It is the same with "renewal," "reconsecration," "rededication," and "revival." One way you look at these four words, they are about the same, and if you are not precise in your thinking you may become impatient with those who insist that they are different. Loosely, they belong to the same general family, but they each offer some slight difference, which may represent some different insight into the way the Holy Spirit works in the lives of believers.

"Dedicate" implies a solemn promise of devotion. It is the moving of the person to put himself at God's disposal. "I dedicate myself to do God's work," one says. "Consecrate" is perhaps a more formal and a more religious word, often used to describe a rite or a ceremony of dedication, as when one consecrates a building or a person to God's service. It denotes a transaction in which man and God are partners. Our fathers used to say, "Man dedicates, God consecrates." Reconsecrate and rededicate simply mean that they are done again.

"Revival" is still different. It comes from the Latin word *vivire* which means to live. The verb form "revive" is probably as old as the English language. William Tyndale used it in 1526 to translate Romans 14:9. "Christ therefore dyed and rose agayne and revived." It means simply "to return to life."

"Revival" as a name for religious movements came into usage about 1700 and has frequently appeared as "revivals of religion." This means a new stirring of God's Spirit in the inner man to bring him back to his former sense of God's presence. Gradually in Baptist usage, the term has come to mean a formal effort to secure a new experience of God's presence more than the actual manifestation of the presence itself. "Revival" is still a good word and should be frequently used; however, we must not be blind to the fact that in some ways it has become a passive word which fails to secure deep personal involvement. This is one reason why some church leaders have turned to "renewal." They find it both new and different.

But "renewal" is not really new; the idea is as old as the Bible. Even John Wycliffe in 1388 used it to translate a biblical idea in 2 Corinthians 4:16, "The ynner man is renewid." It means "to make new again," or in spiritual terms "to recover spiritual life" or "to regenerate." It is new in the sense that it is coming to prominence as a word to describe a spiritual event of the soul. It is certainly different from "reconsecration" or "rededication" or "revival." It is a more personal word and it belongs more to the times. "Rededicate" emphasizes personal decision, "reconsecrate" emphasizes the ceremonial, "revival" suggests re-creating what once was, but "renewal" tells us that the old is being made new. More than the other words, "renewal" carries the force of the biblical idea of regeneration. The plea for renewal is the plea for reformation. It is the bringing of the fire of God back into human life to reestablish the creativity and rejuvenation of the new birth. It is an honest answer to God's truth that "Ye must be born again." Renewal is the recognition that the power and the light of the initial Christian experience must be rekindled again and again until all of life is hallowed.

"Renewal" has been rejected by some because they have thought it strange and unfamiliar, and by others because they have thought it was not a biblical word. They have been surprised to learn that they are wrong. Paul wrote to the Roman Christians, "Be ye transformed by the *renewing* of your mind" (Rom. 12:2). He talked with Titus about "regeneration and *renewing* of the Holy Ghost" (Titus 3:5). He reminded the Corinthian brothers that "the inward man is *renewed* day by day" (2 Cor. 4:16). He pled with the Ephesians to be "*renewed* in the spirit of your mind" (Eph. 4:23). Centuries before Paul used the word, David, the king, prayed, "Create in me a clean heart . . . and *renew* a right spirit within me" (Ps. 51:10). Isaiah said, "They that wait upon the Lord shall *renew* their strength; they shall mount up with wings as eagles" (Isa. 40:31). Can anyone argue that renewal is not a biblical idea?

Renewal can be superficial and effervescent or it can be substantive and life changing. As a fad it is like so much soda pop; once the pressure is off the fizz vanishes. As a vital, life-changing experience, it becomes bread and meat for the daily Christian life, nourishing substance for every vagary and disappointment of life. To be a life-changing experience, renewal must be inspired and nourished by a constant study of God's Word.

The Need for Renewal in the Churches

Renewal is more than a fresh coat of paint or a new steeple. It is more than a stepped-up church program. Too often surface changes are made in the church and everyone feels that it has been renewed. They are surprised to find that nothing short of a spiritual upheaval will truly renew the church.

Before bread can bake light and fluffy in the oven, yeast must do its work. The flour and the water and the shortening and the yeast are kneaded together and the dough is set in a warm, moist place to rise. Millions of tiny yeast pores are born and a sweet fermenting takes place until every molecule of the dough is touched with new life. The dough is literally remade into something different. Renewal has taken place and without it the bread would not be possible.

Too many churches lack the renewing yeast of God's spiritual power. They are cold and dead, living in the past, unwilling to abandon their paralyzing formalities and speaking a contradictory language, singing the ancient and honored language of Zion and shouting the empty shibboleths of modern fads. Many churches have borrowed their agendas both from the past and from the world and have no true voices of their own. As much as at any time in its history, they are being challenged to justify their existence. Either they must prove themselves to be what they say they are, or the world will crowd them off the horizon.

Churches Have Always Been Under Attack

At times churches have appeared to crumble and vanish, yet as history marched on, they have reappeared more vigorous and essen-

24

tial than ever. The world has often been embarrassed and chagrined. In spite of its persecuting and beating these simple fellowships, they often have changed its own face and its own spirit.

What the world has not understood is the power for renewal that rests in the bosom of the churches. It has not fully grasped all the dimensions of the breadth and length and depth and height of the love of Christ which passes all knowledge and which fills the bosom of the churches with all the fulness of God (see Eph. 3:18–19). It does not know the experience of being "strengthened with might by his spirit in the inner man" (Eph. 3:16). The world closes itself to God's Word and misuses the reality of God's kingdom.

Some Churches Are Too Much Like the World

They are like one congregation whose pastor said, "My church is at a low ebb spiritually. We don't really need it, but we've got to build a building to get the members revived." Both pastor and people had fallen to a new low in spiritual life when material things became both the measure and the power of revival. They had developed a great sickness sometimes called "the edifice complex" which acts as if a building is an end within itself. Many earnest church members are finding that a million-dollar auditorium built so well that it could be turned on its side and rolled across a mountain without breaking apart does not automatically bring a great church spirit or a strong congregational vitality. In fact, it may actually bring church depression, for the reason that in the midst of the fever to build the building the true sense of churchly mission is lost.

This statement is not meant to condemn adequate and beautiful buildings or any of the other material possessions of the churches, such as air conditioners, yellow buses, gymnasiums, parking lots, robed choirs, stainless steel kitchens, and padded pews. These all have their place, but they are not to be substituted for the Holy Spirit. They can be useful to present-day churches, but they are not to be bought at the cost of losing the power that makes a church a church, the indwelling presence of Christ.

Deep, vital life renewal is the only thing that will restore the sense of churchly balance. This comes when church members begin a deep and earnest study of the Bible, and when they rededicate their lives wholly to Christ. It continues only as they share God's Word with the whole world. Only with Christ in their hearts and the Scriptures in their testimony can they have power for their mission to lost mankind. In the Bible they find not only the renewal of the inner man, but their mandate for existence.

Some Churches Exist Without a Sense of Mission

They see themselves only as shelters of refuge where a few people gather on weekends, and not caring whether the masses ever join with them in their worship and study. Here again we must be very careful not to leave the impression that these gatherings are unimportant. The exact opposite is true—they are supremely important. The point here is that the meaning has gone out of some of the gatherings because they have been allowed to become ends within themselves. For their members, the chief value of church is found in simply going to church.

The hard truth is that if the attending is to survive, it must be seen as leading to something. For most churches this means the reawakening of their sense of uniqueness in the world and of their awareness of responsibility for the world. They will once more see themselves as the people of God and as the salt of the earth. They will see what surely can be seen on every street and in every home—that the world is lost and needs saving. They will declare to the whole world, every country of it, that only Jesus Christ can save.

Unless churches are gripped by this simple mission, attendance will die and the edifices will become mausoleums of the past. How do churches see themselves as the salt of the earth? And where do they get their mandate and motivation for mission? From the Scriptures. It is in the Bible that the church sees itself as the body of Christ and the bride of Christ and realizes it is responsible for sharing Christ and his Word with the whole world.

No Church Can Survive Nourished Only on the Victories of the Past

It is good to remember the great revivals of long ago and to recall the outpourings of God's Spirit in other days. These remind us of what is surely true. The churches are born out of great upsurging of spiritual renewal, and they are sustained by the recurring visitations of the Holy Spirit. But mere memory is never enough. Simply recalling a love long dead does not rekindle the fires on the hearth of the home.

Love to be real must be present now. The spiritual life of a church to be real must also be present now. Renewal is concerned with this one thing, the rediscovery of the spiritual dimension in church membership. It is the reassertion of God's presense in human life and the rekindling of his fire in the human heart by the reading and the living of the Word of God. One cannot study the New Testament without being impressed by the inner working of God's Spirit in human experience. Jesus said, "I will pray the Father, and he shall give you another Comforter, that he may abide with you for ever; even the Spirit of truth . . . for he *dwelleth with you, and shall be in you*" (John 14:16–17).

The church is alive only as the reality of God in Christ is a present real experience in the lives of the church members. Paul said, "Examine yourselves, to see whether you are holding to your faith. Test yourselves. Do you not realize that Jesus Christ is in you?—Unless indeed you fail to meet the test" (2 Cor. 13:5, RSV). Renewal in the churches will come only as church members look deeply into the New Testament and ask themselves, "Is Christ truly within us? Are we truly Christian now?"

Some Churches Sometimes Are Darker on the Inside than the World Is on the Outside

One suspects that one reason so many youth have left us is that they thought that there was little or no joy in the church, no festivity, no sense of celebration, no grappling with vital life problems, no mingling of the ages, no deep friendships between the generations, and above all, no spiritual mystery. Of course they are wrong, for they are the sad ones who sense something dead in their own lives and project their lack upon others. They frantically search for life in all kinds of physical and social excesses, floundering on the slippery roof of sin, and finally falling into the pit of complete selfishness. For them the inner light of the church is the light that failed.

Why did the light fail for them? Perhaps for two reasons: First they did not realize that God is speaking personally to them from the Scriptures. They were told about the Bible, but they were not taught the Bible so that it became for them an intimate knowledge of God, and they did not commit themselves to Jesus Christ. The written Word and the personal Word did not become in their lives an indissoluble experience. Second they did not find a true sense of fellowship in the church. It was a place to go, and for them a miserable experience, because those in leadership took entirely too much for granted. The youth missed the Light because the lower lights did not shine brightly enough.

The Lower Lights Must Burn More Brightly

Clyde Reid in *The God-Evaders* has said that too often religious organizations and religious leaders reject spiritually sensitive people. He points to the spiritual poverty in our church fellowship as proof, "Speak to the average church officer today and you will discover that he has little awareness of his denomination's history or beliefs, little religious conviction, often doubts the existence of God. And sadly, he has had to carry on a smiling deception in regard to his doubts, for his church has never allowed him an opportunity to admit them honestly and to work them through. Or speak to a group of church people about the power of silent prayer and observe their discomfort. Observe a deacons' meeting in some church and note the perfunctory opening prayer, simply a curtsy in the direction of God, bereft of relevance or power for those listening." [1]

What is wrong here? The truth is that faith is not a vital life value for some church members. They have heard that without faith it is impossible to please God, but they have never really heeded it. They continue loyal to the institution of the church, without any great sense of commitment to Christ.

We must admit we have a problem at this point, and that the church is up against an unbelieving and unfriendly world. Churches with the open Bible constantly in the hands of their members do not seem to be discouraged as much as churches who treat the Scriptures as an incidental decoration. A Bible-centered church is more than a gathering of casual acquaintances; it is a fellowship of friends in Christ. Sharing the Word with each other will strengthen the vitality and will prepare the members for the discouragement the church faces from the world.

Asking an Egg and Getting a Scorpion

No one, not even he who is least observant, can ignore the revolutions taking place in the world. A new man and a new society are forming. On the one hand we see a man of greater knowledge taking his place in a society of greater freedom. On the other hand, we see a man whose hopes and dreams are threatened by the social evils of massive world war and racial hatred.

The churches can accept this in two ways—one that it offers extreme danger, the other that it offers highest opportunity. Gibson Winter has said that the present, in terms of opportunity for Christians, is to be compared with the first few centuries of the Christian era, the twelfth century in Western Europe or the century of the Reformation.

Perhaps our church opportunities are increased because of the great unanswered hunger of mankind. Man has tasted the arts and the sciences, to find them fascinating and worthy of life dedication, but unsatisfying to the needs of the soul. He has tasted democracy and found it good, only to learn that it did not contain the spiritual vitamins of basic life need. He has tasted communism to find it an empty husk, war to find it a burning coal in his belly, narcotics to find them poison, alcohol to find it a whistle in the wind. He has asked the world for a fish and got a snake, for an egg and got a scorpion, for bread and got a stone. Frustrated and empty man now turns to the churches and asks, "What have you to give?"

In one breath the modern man dismisses the churches as so much garbage, in another he begs them for help. "If you are really the leaven of God, then leaven me," he cries. "If you have the water of life, then give me to drink. If you are the salt of the earth, then let me taste your savor. If you are the light of the world, then shine on me." The answer is not merely another attendance plan or visitation campaign, another building or another series of newspaper ads as essential as these things are.

The answer is genuine spiritual renewal, not a new paint job or a new carpet, but church renewal born out of personal renewal. It is in new life that comes when every member lives to the fullest the indwelling of Jesus Christ. It is the Scriptures breaking anew in our hearts, the burning of our lives as Christ comes to us from his Word.

As Moffatt translated Paul's words, "Do you not understand that Christ Jesus is within you? Otherwise you must be failures" (2 Cor. 13:5).

The Need for Personal Renewal

Some church members are tired, and feel that all excitement and inspiration have gone out of their Christian experience. Some pastors complain that church jobs are harder to fill, and that families who were once loyal are now completely disinterested. One pastor reported that in one year's time, four families formerly active in the church had now completely severed all ties. One of these families when visited during the church budget drive said: "Oh, I used to go, but now I've found a new freedom."

What is wrong here? Is it really the church? Or is it people? Of course, it is both. As personal interest and involvement decline, the congregation grows weaker. Instead of directing our appeals for renewal broadly to the church, we should direct them to individual church members. We should realize that after all only as individuals are renewed can the church be renewed.

The signs of decline in personal interest are at first hard to see. One of them is that the inner circle of the church grows smaller. People formerly close to it or part of it are nowhere near to it now. Prayer meetings become lifeless, business meetings poorly attended and even deacons' meetings a drag. Another is that people refuse to take responsibility for the religious education of the young. Simple teaching jobs go unfilled, and some parents even raise doubts about the importance of religious education. Still another sign is that tithes and offerings decline, missions go unsupported and bills unpaid.

The least heeded signs are that there is no vitality for the sharing of faith; and that evangelism as a viable church enterprise disappears with some Christians even doubting its importance.

The tragedy of these signs is that they can exist for years. People can be half in and half out of the church, not realizing that at the bottom is the lack of personal commitment. This can happen even to ministers.

One of the most graphic pictures of personal spiritual destitution is given by Elton Trueblood in *Your Other Vocation*. He says of a church meeting: "There was no surprise, no novelty, no real beauty or dignity, and consequently very little attention. It was as though an old record, worn by much use, were being run again and no one seemed to have any clear reason for running it. The hymns were sung, not because some great testimony was being jointly made, but because hymn singing was the conventional thing to do, and the prayers were given, not because of inner compulsion, but because praying was expected." [2]

One does not renew the worship service with a new set of hymns or with a new sequence of the parts. Real renewal begins with people, specifically with persons, with individuals whose minds will change and whose hearts will quicken. It takes place deep in the inner life of man with the revival of the soul by a fresh infilling of God's Spirit. It starts with a fervent rededication to the Word of God. Genuine Bible study will bring any Christian a deeper appreciation of his own salvation experience.

Harry Schiensburg, now an effective missionary in South America, was an aimless young man in Australia when a stranger thrust a New Testament into his hands. He began at once to read and was soon converted. This led to an intensive study of the Bible, and to a life rich and diverse in its service to God and man. In Brazil a farmer was given a Scripture portion. He found it so compelling that he rode a horse fifty miles to find someone to tell him what it meant. George Herbert said, "Bibles laid open millions of surprises." Personal study of the Bible inevitably leads to the enrichment of life and to a greater understanding of what it means to be in unison with Christ.

A New Sense of Fellowship

Revival of fellowship is one of the most difficult problems faced by the local church, and it will not be solved until individual church members see themselves as responsible. Intensive study of the New Testament will clear up some misconceptions about fellowship.

First it will show us that the gospel does not call for us to lose ourselves in the group. Leaders sometimes say this in order to make the point of needed involvement, but Jesus never said or did anything to destroy individuality. He did call for his disciples to die as a grain of wheat and live again in the new creation, but not to the place that Peter would be someone else or John someone altogether different. His point was personal redemption and not substitution of human individuality. What he emphasized was individual human freedom, responsible personal trust and personal honesty in being oneself. Christian fellowship is the friendly relationship of greatly different personalities in an atmosphere of freedom and trust, not a false masking of all people until they look like so many identical cans on the self.

Second, study of the Bible will show us that Christian fellowship is not all there is to the life of the church. Many modern Christian writers like Peter Berger seem to equate church and fellowship, even to the point of seeing no good in present church structures. This is extreme, yet important as fellowship may be, it is nothing unless it also engages in worship, evangelism, missions, Christian education and many other equally important things.

Third, a study of the Bible will show us that true fellowship is not mere "togetherness." Leaving a church picnic one person said, "I enjoyed the *koinonia*." Speaking of that same picnic another said, "I was miserable the whole time." Everyone was equally present but everyone was not equally in fellowship. Regarding *koinonia* (New Testament Greek for "fellowship") we make two mistakes. On the one hand, we don't have enough church picnics, and on the other hand, we sum up such things as *koinonia*. In true *koinonia*, it is essential for one to be in fellowship with both God and man.

Fourth, careful study of God's Word shows us that true fellowship is fellowship in the *gospel*, not in the *church*. One simply cannot induce fellowship from church suppers and weekend retreats. These are necessary and will overflow from fellowship. The source of true New Testament community is Christ and his love for man. It is impossible in the church to have fellowship without the gospel.

Fifth, a study of God's Word shows us that true fellowship does not exist for its own sake. A dynamo is a magnificent piece of machinery, but unless its power is sent over wires to distant homes and factories, it really has no justification for its existence. New Testament fellowship soon dies out unless its members take a servant role to all mankind, as disciples of Christ in an estranged and distraught world.

What does this mean for the individual? How can he lay hold of fellowship as a viable part of his own life? Where are the handles? An alcoholic in an AA meeting said: "I lived for forty years without wanting any of the finer things of life or without being associated with better people. I wanted no part of it." He never saw himself moving into a better life until he felt deep within a great need which could be filled only with what the group had to offer.

It may be the same with Christians. Not until they see and feel vital Christian fellowship as the vital air they breathe, can they really become committed to it. This comes sometimes at the end of desperation, as one feels the lack of nourishment in the empty husks he is eating. It comes as a result of a study of the Bible from which we learn the nature and the need of the fellowship. Mostly it comes as other members of Christ, prompted by the Word of God and acting as his agents of reconciliation begin to close the gaps between themselves and the estranged ones. One young man, reared in the church, but long at war with it, after trying everything else, was pulled back into the fellowship by loving arms. He cried, "Thank God, I am home again." Once having tasted the true fellowship of the gospel, there is nothing else to take its place.

A New Sense of Mystery

Paul wrote of "the fellowship of the mystery" (Eph. 3:9). He said also that as Christians "We speak the wisdom of God in a mystery, even the hidden wisdom of God" (1 Cor. 2:7). He said bishops should hold "the mystery of the faith in a pure conscience" (2 Tim. 3:9). He wrote to the Romans of "the revelation of the mystery, which was kept secret since the world began" (Rom. 16:25). In ancient classical Greek usage "mystery" meant "secret." Paul's use of it made it mean "open secret." This is suggested in Ephesians 3:3,5: "How that by revelation he made known unto me the mystery . . . which in other ages was not made known unto the sons of men, as it is now revealed unto his holy apostles and prophets by the Spirit." One must remember that it is still an open secret, open to believers, closed to unbelievers.

The mystery is still present. In fact there are many mysteries, among them the mystery of the holding together of the body of Christ, the mystery of the indwelling Christ in the hearts of believers, the mystery of the regenerative power of God's Holy Spirit, the mystery of the resurrection of Christ, and the mystery of the promised resurrection of all believers. These are the ineffaceable mysteries which cannot be explained away. Whoever comes to Christ comes to mystery which he must accept by faith. The Bible makes this very clear.

God in his Book has told us many things but not everything, knowing that these strange earthly creatures of his live by mystery. It is the unknown that challenges man and it is the glimmer of the glow in the unknown that pulls him forward. The Bible itself is a book of unfolding mystery, showing us the mysteries of God.

F. Dean Lueking in his discussion of the local church in *The Future of the Christian World Mission* tells of a young man who had been on drugs who came to see him and asked if he had thirty minutes for meditation. "Wanting to show me what he does each day, he opened his guitar case, set upon my desk an eight by ten picture of an Indian mystic, and took out a paper back on the discipline of the inner life. Then he proceeded to put me out of his mind and concentrate on guitar chords, incantations, and the gentle compulsion of those eyes peering at him from the photograph." [3] Mr. Lueking makes the point that this young man is one of many in the world who is looking for inner illumination by turning to Eastern mysticism.

Not all people are so extreme in their search for mystery, but all to one degree or other are searching. The most satisfying of all mysteries is the mystery of God coming to man in Christ. Taste that mystery of God and you are forever satisfied, refuse it and you are always hungry. One replies, "But I cannot abandon myself to believe in that mystery. It is not reasonable." Then we must say back to him, "You have missed the mystery of mysteries, the open secret of God's love, for without faith to believe, the mystery always remains secret. Unbelievers cannot possibly share the mystery." We must somehow lead the unbeliever into a personal knowledge of the Word, and to see that abandonment to the mystery of God's love is essential to personal renewal.

A New Sense of Uniqueness

We need to face it—true Christians are different. Their discovery of this difference may mark their renewal in the Christian life.

One cannot read the New Testament without sensing the unique position of the followers of Christ. Jesus called them his brothers and his sisters, the sheep of his fold, the sons of God, the ones given to him by the Father, the salt of the earth. He said that the hairs of their heads are numbered and that their names are written in heaven. They are the possessors of the spirit of truth, the ones who look for that blessed hope, and who are promised a crown of righteousness on the day of judgment. They are "the elect according to the foreknowledge of God" (1 Pet. 1:2). They are "as lively stones . . . built up a spiritual house, . . . to offer up spiritual sacrifices, acceptable to God by Jesus Christ" (1 Pet. 2:5). They are "a chosen generation, a royal priesthood, an holy nation, a peculiar people . . . the people of God" (1 Pet. 2:9–10). Christ has made them "priests and kings unto God his Father" (Rev. 1:6).

These high honors are not merely for the adornment of the Christian, as so often they have been misinterpreted, but to prepare him to be a burden-bearer and a servant. They mark him as unique among people, as different in calling, different in character, different in work, and different in destiny. A discovery of this uniqueness can lead one to a renewal of his entire Christian outlook. It can transform him from a wooden do-nothing and be-nothing into a shouting member of God's community.

A New Sense of Servanthood

People who attended the Baptist World Congress in Brazil in 1955 were astonished to find so many Baptists among hotel chambermaids and porters. They found that in Brazil being a Christian meant absolute honesty and that these people were greatly sought by hotel managers as a protection for their guests. The point here is not that being a Christian makes us the lackeys of the world, but that being Christian makes one a peacemaker and a healer in a world broken by hatred and sin. If we are truly Christian, our new nature will make us stand out in contrast against the crude and wicked people of the world. We will be true servants of all mankind.

Jesus surely stressed this serving and caring role for his disciples. One way of looking at it is that he showed he was much more concerned about the renewal of the world than he did about the renewal of the church. It was for the world that he died, and it was for the world he expected his disciples to live, not as belonging to the world, but as belonging to him. He saw quite clearly that full manhood involves both personal and social responsibility, and requires every man to realize his own uniqueness as a servant of God to the world. The teaching of the leaven in the meal imposes upon the Christian frightening responsibility.

The easiest thing for the Christian to do is to retreat into the solid stone walls of the church, refusing to take his place as a Christian citizen. When he does this, he becomes a faceless automaton in a society he was meant to change. He becomes a dead and lifeless spore, and the world is denied his yeast. A mean and unlovely man was married to a lovely girl. Both were circus people. Finally, the girl wanted to leave him. A wise old clown then asked her if she did not love him and stay with him, who would? This is the question for the Christian. "If you don't stay with the world and its need, who will?"

The terrible obligation that Christian servanthood places upon us can be seen in the simple word, "cup." When Jesus used this word, he meant his death and his crucifixion. He asks two questions, "Can you drink of this cup?" "Will you drink of it?" And he reminds us, "Greater love hath no man than this, that a man will lay down his life for his friends" (John 16:13). For Jesus this meant action, a visit to a prison, a stay in a sick room, a piece of bread for the hungry, a kind word for the stranger and a cup of cold water for the thirsty.

The servanthood he places upon us is an everyday servanthood, one that leads us to minister to the people near at hand. Of course, our Lord is interested in our expedition to the other side of the railroad track, and he wants us to organize to reach the slums, but his big interest is in our being a servant beginning in our own home, and going on to our daily work. Surely he is not happy about the so-called prophetic statements of men who live in mansions and drive elegant cars but never bother to wash the poor man's soiled linen or to be a friend to a sick alcoholic. Nor is he too happy abut do-goodism or theoretical ethics. He is deeply concerned about the quality of life that makes good neighbors.

I believe we are on the verge of a new Pentecost, one in which God's Holy Spirit will move Christians to witness through their servanthood to all mankind. The winds are blowing, the churches are changing, the Spirit is moving, renewal is taking place, and we see persons becoming concerned for each other. A new ministry of reconciliation is about to take place. Renewal of Bible study shows the way.

Consider the little word "seek." What a marvelous storehouse of Christian thought and understanding. "Seek ye first the kingdom of God" (Matt. 6:33). "Seek, and ye shall find" (Matt. 7:7). Consider also the word "study." "Study to show thyself approved" (2 Tim. 2:15). And consider the word "search." "Search the scriptures; for in them ye think ye have eternal life" (John 5:39). Now look at the word "ask." "Ask, and it shall be given you" (Matt. 7:7). And finally look at "pray." "Lord, teach us to pray" (Luke 11:1). "Pray without ceasing" (1 Thess. 5:17). "Pray, lest ye enter into temptation" (Luke 22:46).

"Seek," "ask," "study," "search," "pray"—all these words belong together. They call for the open mind and open heart, and they mark the truly alive and influential Christian. The churches are deadest and emptiest when all the seeking and the searching go out of the lives of its members, and when they act as if there were no new thing to be learned, no new feeling to be experienced, no new insight to be gained.

The failure to seek, to ask, to study, to search, to pray is the failure to dream dreams and see visions. It is the sign of empty, dead, spiritless Christian lives. Because of this failure churches are clouds without rain, cisterns without water, and trees without fruit.

How does this tragedy happen?

1. For one thing, because of poor spiritual leadership. One pastor prays in such a way that some of his members go to sleep. His preaching is in a dull conversational tone that betrays his lack of enthusiasm for his material. There is no timbre of mission and challenge in his voice. He rarely speaks with urgency and never challenges his listeners to responsibility. His appeal for involvement is tacked onto a sermon as an afterthought and either is highly irrelevant to the world or just as irrelevant to the Bible. He never has learned to bring the word and the Word together.

2. Another reason is our failure to see the whole Bible as relevant to life. The Bible's meaning is for now, even for today's world of science and materialism, and capable of demonstrating itself as an immensely practical book, if only we are open to its message.

Harvey Cox in the book *God's Revolution and Man's Responsibility* helps us see that we need to accept the whole counsel of God as immediately relevant and practical for our most secular needs. "Theologians need to engage not so much in demythalogizing as in despiritualizing the Bible. The best way to do this is to stand with one foot in the Old Testament and one foot in the political struggle of our world today. From this dual standpoint, one can examine what God is saying to modern man in the New Testament." [4] The Bible is an immensely practical book and holds the answer to the world's ills.

3. A third reason is that we have stylized the Christian experience, reducing it to a rite and a ceremony, and not seeing it as embracing the whole of life. This may be due to a lack of understanding of what the Bible teaches about conversion. A young man gives his girl an engagement ring, and she says, "Yes, I will marry you." The ring is not the end of meaning, no matter if it cost a million dollars. The true meaning transcends the ceremony and is deeply seated in the endless possibilities of relationships as they live together in freedom. The meaning transcends the moment of the ceremony and extends to the whole of life. There is no end to it, as long as the two of them remain alive and in relationship to each other.

One man, married to the same woman for thirty-five years, is astounded at the new revelations that come as he seeks earnestly to understand his wife. As long as he is blind, he sees nothing new, but with eyes and heart open, all things become new. He feels far richer now than he did the day of the engagement—simply because all these years he has been a seeker. The Bible helps us keep our eyes open to Christian experience.

The Christian life is far more than a Sunday morning walk down the church aisle or a fleeting experience of baptism. If these stylized experiences are all that there are to it—and one feels that for a great many people this is the case—then the Christian life is nothing. The glory of the Christian life is in the seeking of Christian meaning for the whole of life. If Christians can be led to do this, the church will be a whole new "ball game"—to use a fairly well-known phrase from the streets.

This, of course, is renewal, and renewal is essential to tomorrow's church. But let us remember that we are not talking here about renewal that next year has to be repeated again, or renewal that storms the emotions without strengthening the will. Such renewal is dry grass that soon disappears. We are talking about bedrock renewal that is only possible as man feeds his soul on the Word of God, as renewal that finds its fire in the church learning the Word, and sharing the Word with all mankind.

3] [Teaching the Word

One of today's beautiful people with long blonde hair, faded blue jeans and tie-dyed shirt was heard to say that she was going to an "excitement." She was on her way to a lively and happy party. Later when her pastor showed more than usual enthusiasm in his sermon she said, "It was an excitement." The service had caught her interest and for a time she lived outside herself in a social and spiritual transcendence; momentarily she escaped the dullness which she felt threatened her life.

It is a paradox of the times that in spite of the ever-present television and ubiquitous spectator sports, man finds or seems to find little to make his life exciting. Passive entertainment, no matter how good it may be, never completely satisfies his need for involvement. If his work does not satisfy him, he will turn to something else. He will do what offers him the most excitement.

Long ago man had to dig wells and hunt animals for a living. With the threat of a well caving in on him or a bear chasing him up a tree, he did not need planned excitements as man does today when the worst thing that can happen is for the faucet to leak or the cat get sick. Add to this the dullness of most contemporary jobs and you have a picture of what drives so many people up the wall, with some slipping into physical excesses such as drugs and violence. Even if they do not become extremists or exhibitionists, they still measure the quality of life by how much excitement it offers.

Modern man is not likely to submit again soon to the monotony of life that reached its peak in the fifties when everyone looked and dressed alike, when for most people there was just one life-style. One must admit that the varieties of haircuts and beards today may not always be neat and appealing, but they are certainly not dull.

It just may be that most people seek excessive excitement not to satisfy or feed self, but to escape self. Whatever the reason, excite-

40

ment will be with us for a long time to come. Strange as it may seem to some, we must make it part of the Christian learning experience if we are to survive.

The dullness of some Sunday Schools is appalling. The quality most lacking is enthusiasm. In one church the man at the door extends a cold, arthritic hand and frowns if you exert the slightest pressure. The halls are filled with people who don't know quite where to go, or maybe don't want to. The Sunday School assembly rooms have a scattering of people, quiet and sober, like waiting for a funeral to begin. When the service starts, there is a feeble question, "What shall we sing?" After a long pause and no answer the leader says, "Let's sing 'Love Lifted Me.' This is a key the pianist can play." Then follows a series of dull announcements, and people go stifly off to their classes. The Sunday School teacher drones on and on, never relating his truth to people. If someone asks him a question, it scares him to death.

Sunday morning Bible study can be dull for a variety of reasons:

(1) We fail to make the connection between the Bible and life.

(2) We forget the Holy Spirit is alive in our presence.

(3) We mistake formality for reverence.

(4) We create an impossible learning situation by eliminating all dialogue.

(5) We slavishly stay with set routines.

(6) We create a sterile fellowship by eliminating all age mix.

(7) We do not make room for fellowship either in our procedures or our building arrangements.

(8) We refuse to learn how to communicate to the world in modern terms and with modern means.

(9) We don't want to offend anyone with a positive and emphatic gospel.

(10) We feel it is not nice or polite to be enthusiastic in our teaching.

(11) We hide the fact that Christians are a people set apart from the world.

(12) We do not use imagination.

Bible teaching does not have to be dull. One of the most exciting Bible teachers I ever knew was R. C. Howard, Sr., of Oklahoma City. When he opened the Bible, the people who listened believed that something was going to happen. He was a lay preacher, but he knew how to make the Bible live.

One memorable lesson was from Paul's passages on family life and marriage. Before he finished he had turned the meeting into a three-way dialogue between himself, his congregation, and the Scriptures on what family life really means.

One thing that made Kelham Avenue Bible study a spiritual excitement in those days was the unpredictability of R. C. Howard. He was so resourceful that nobody could guess what he would do, so they went to find out. His greatest visible contribution was his enthusiasm. When he took the podium, he exuded authentic enthusiasm, not a sham enthusiasm for enthusiasm's sake, but a real enthusiasm for his Bible message. He was actually a very dignified man and wore a red carnation every day.

The Excitement of the Material for Bible Study

"Nobody gets excited about the Bible anymore," a cynical pastor was heard to say at his state convention. When pressed, he admitted he was not excited. His preaching, he said, was drawn mostly from magazines and newspapers. The man is a dolt in the pulpit.

Contrast his attitude with that of another pastor who had to buy a new Bible because he had worn out the Gospel of John. In fact he has several such Bibles with "worn-out" books. Isaiah, the Psalms, Romans, the minor prophets, among them. He finds the Bible exciting enough to wear out in constant study. He is past eighty years old and still in wide demand as a Bible teacher. There is nothing weak or listless about this preacher. Listening to him is to get the feeling that the Bible is the most exciting book in the world.

Lay teachers also find the Bible exciting in its content. John Gifford, a businessman and a major general in the Air Force Reserve, is one of them. He has studied the Bible so exhaustively and so carefully and has found so many ways to relate it to life that listening to him in a Sunday School class is to take a seat on front row of a theater in which the great events of God reaching out for man are taking place. One feels the thunders of Sinai and the thirst of Golgotha. To hear him teach the resurrection of Christ is to stand finally before the open tomb and say, "He is alive!" John Gifford can do this because he believes the Bible is a book as much relevant to the needs of the men of today as it was to the needs of men who lived when it was first written. He is no sissy either.

It is not uncommon to hear people say, "For the first time in life I am really reading the Bible" in such a way as to learn the impressions that "For the first time I am beginning to see the Bible for what it really is and I am deeply moved for what I read." Suddenly for them, due to some catalyzing experience the Bible has become an excitement. In its pages they find themselves and their dilemmas, and quite to their surprise, they find also the way out of their problems.

The Bible Has Human Appeal

Read the first three chapters of Genesis in a fresh, new translation and feel once more your personal involvement in the creation story. Put a copy of *The Living Bible, Paraphrased* in the hands of a teenager and ask him to tell you what he sees and feels when he reads the story of Ruth and Naomi. He may cry out, "Boy, that was an excitement." Read the story of the prodigal son to a man in prison and ask him what it makes him think about. You may hear even the most sadistic and selfish sinner say that he wants to go home and begin all over again. Read him the miracles and the parables from *Today's English Version,* and you will awaken him to a whole new world of spiritual understanding in which he begins to find himself.

Earthquakes, rainstorms, floods, fires, famines, diseases, droughts, wars—these are very human experiences and the Bible is full of them. Anger, hatred, envy, jealousy, love, kindness, loyalty, deception, madness—these human emotions are also present in the Bible, and validate it as an authentic human book in tune with the thoughts and experiences of men. The ax that floats, the fish that swallows a man, the waters that divide, the replenished oil in the pitcher, the boat big enough for all creation, the water turned into wine, the empty tomb, the ascension of Christ into heaven—these are the ear-stunning miracles of the Bible that give it universal human appeal.

A man lingered in front of a book store window in Alexandria, Egypt. His eye was fastened on an open book on display. It was a New Testament in large print and open at Luke 15, the story of the prodigal son. Inside he asked to buy the book. "This is my own story," he told the clerk. "I took my father's money and went to Europe and Lebanon, but I didn't find peace and rest. Finally I decided to come back." The man left with the book, deeply moved with the Word of God.

The Literary Charm of the Bible

I have a friend who taught English in one of America's great colleges. After he had been retired several months, I went one morning to call on him. He met me at the door with a beautiful book in hand. "Prof, what are you doing?" I asked him. He quickly replied, "As you know, I love the English language, and to me the King James Version of the Bible is the most beautiful book in English. On these long days when I am alone I will read aloud to myself sometimes as much as an hour. This morning I have been reading the book of Job."

My old professor long ago had conveyed to me the charm of the Bible. He taught his classes sitting on a high stool. I can still hear him now reading from his pedestal in his strong velvet voice the twenty-third Psalm or the Lord's Prayer. When he read the Scriptures, they held new meaning for me. I think it was because he knew by instinct their great charm and beauty.

Too many Bible teachers are sloppy in the way they read the Bible aloud, and what comes through is a stammering succession of broken phrases, with little coherence and unity, and with nothing pleasing to the ear of the listener. The charm of how the Bible sounds is lost, and with it some of the meaning is lost.

The Moral Challenge of the Bible

Many life-changing books have been written, but none as timeless and as universal as the Bible. William Cowper said that "It gives a light to ev'ry age." Richard Crashaw called it "an armoury of light." The psalmist felt its moral impact: "Thy word is a lamp unto my feet, and a light unto my path" (Ps. 119:105). Paul put it: "All scripture . . . is profitable for doctrine, for reproof, for correction, for instruction in righteousness" (2 Tim. 3:16).

There was once a young man who sat on his father's front porch, really reading the Bible for the first time in his life. He had read at it many times and knew many of its stories and sayings, but he had never before heard it speaking to him. As he read, every word became an unbearable spiritual burden. It was as though God was speaking to him directly from the pages. Every phrase held both condemnation and hope. The weight became so heavy that he laid the book aside and literally ran to get away from it. He took a long walk through the town pondering its meaning.

Finally he was drawn back to the Bible, and as he read he saw more hope than condemnation. In the backyard under a peach tree that had lost its leaves in a September drought and with a full moon overhead he surrendered himself wholly and completely to God. The moral challenge of the Bible had made the difference. The words he had been reading were the words of Jesus from the Sermon on the Mount: "And every one who heareth these sayings of mine, and doeth them not, shall be likened unto a foolish man which built his house upon the sand: and the rain descended, and the floods came, and the winds blew, and beat upon that house; and it fell: and great was the fall of it" (Matt. 7:26–27).

The Bible as a Story of Divine Redemption

Exciting as the Bible is in its human appeal, its literary charm, and its moral challenge, there is no excitement as great as its story of God's search for man and the salvation offered him. There is an indelible line written on almost every page, and that moves unbroken from God's loving creation of man to his final acceptance into heaven. That line says over and over again, "God is love."

Steve Driggers is a Georgia man who joined the army and went to Vietnam. Like many others he drifted into drugs, first marijuana, then heroin. He said, "Seeing the crippled, wounded, and dying caused me to look for an escape from reality. Heroin seemed the easiest way." He bickered, he argued, he became incompetent and selfish. He lived from one "fix" to another. "Suddenly I realized I no longer believed even in God. I seemed to be on an absolute collision course."

He entered the drug amnesty program but did not make a clean break. Marijuana still had a strong hold on him. He deceived his superiors and served as a drug counselor while still smoking pot. Morally he was at the bottom when he began to read *Good News for Modern Man*. A chaplain explained Christ to him. "As we talked I became convinced that someone did care and that my life could be different. . . . I sincerely asked for forgiveness, peace, and direction. Christ heard my prayers. By faith I reached out and accepted his forgiveness and love. Today I am no longer dependent on drugs. . . . Because of what Christ and His Word have done in my life, I am now a very happy young man." Like the Chinese who wrote his American friend, "I am reading the Bible and behaving it," Steve Driggers has found the Word of God an excitement that he says will carry him through college and seminary and into the ministry.[1]

> O teach us Lord, thy living Word
> > Enduring truth, renewing light
> In ages past it stood the test
> > And long survived the pagan night
> O teach us, Lord, to search thy Word
> > And break the chains of stilted creeds
> > Let man be still, give God his say.

The Excitement of Preparation

Saturday night is the worst time of all to begin preparation to teach a Sunday School lesson. What comes out the next morning will be dull, inaccurate, and perhaps even unrelated to the lesson. A serious teacher will begin early in the week and build not only his knowledge of the lesson, but his enthusiasm for it. When a teacher begins his class by saying, "This is a very dull lesson," or "The quarterlies don't tell me anything about this lesson," get set for a boring forty-five minutes. It means that he is uninformed and without much interest. There can only be excitement in the classroom where there has been excitement in the teacher's preparation.

Preparation can be exciting provided one enters seriously into a step-by-step plan to make the lesson live in his own life and then in the lives of the believers: (1) Read the passage over and over again until you can visualize it completely from beginning to end. Read the larger lesson, and read it in several different versions. This should be done very early in the week.

(2) Become completely acquainted with all the characters and places mentioned in the text. A good Bible dictionary will help you do this, as well as the quarterlies your church furnishes for you. Meet the characters as friends and the places as though you were on a journey.

(3) Begin early in the week to ask, "What has this lesson got to

do with the people in my class in their life and times of the 1970's?" As you mull the lesson, it will surprise you how many ways it can be related to your daily experiences.

(4) Read all the quarterlies and any other commentary you can find that will help you develop as a Bible student. Your denomination produces the very best literature available. The person who complains about it has surely not seriously studied it, for unequaled scholarship and dedication go into its preparation.

(5) Attend your weekly teachers' meeting where the lesson is being taught for teachers. Dialogue with others who also must teach the lesson the next Sunday will stretch your imagination and fill your cup. The dialogue itself will be an excitement and you will look forward to Sunday instead of dreading it.

(6) Make a lesson plan. You can begin by examining the lesson plans in your teacher's guide. Sometimes you can use these. Sometimes you can't, but they are always useful in helping you to develop your own. It is surprising what a lesson plan will do to help you tie the lesson and life together. It does not have to be complicated or detailed, only reflective of you and your enthusiasm.

(7) Begin your Sunday as quietly and devotionally as you can. For you the lesson will start with your morning prayers. If your household duties keep you from spending another hour with your lesson alone, pray and think as you work.

(8) Arrive early at the church. Part of the excitement of Sunday Bible study is meeting the class one by one as they arrive. You begin teaching with the first warm hello.

Great Bible teachers are made during the week, not on Sunday. They are made out of long, hard study of the Bible and the constant effort to relate its truth to life. They are made out of men and women who love the Bible and who love people. An exciting teacher on Sunday is one who has found excitement in his study during the week.

The Excitement of the Classroom

Dull teachers make dull students, but what makes dull teachers? Or to ask the question another way, "What brings dull teachers to life?" Important as detailed preparation is to good Bible teaching, some of the dullest teachers are the best prepared. We sometimes describe them as overprepared, but this is wrong, because long hours of study are not all there is to preparation. The best preparation is involvement with people in continuing conversation about life and its problems.

The dullest teacher is often one who has all the facts clearly in mind but none of the fire because he is not close enough to the great problems of life to be sensitive to the needs of his people. This kind of teacher is more comfortable with the lecture method of teaching because it is the least disturbing to him. He feels safer when talking alone about the events of the past than he does in talking together about the effect of those events in the present. Most teachers who teach like this, teach for their own sakes, not for the sake of others. This makes Sunday School a boring experience for too many people. The teacher is dull because of his general noninvolvement in life; he can be bright as he begins to see life as a dialogue.

Rice Pierce in his helpful book, *Leading Dynamic Bible Study,* wrote, "The Scriptures can be studied in a ceremonial mechanical, dull, now-we-are-in-Sunday-School manner. Or you—the teacher —and the class members may study the Bible in a dynamic manner. You and your class may plumb the very depths of mind and heart, together, as you seek to know and do God's will through study of the written revelation. This spiritual experience may be called *dynamic Bible study.* "

Plumbing the Depths of Mind and Heart—Together

Excitement begins in the classroom when both teacher and pupils begin to realize that they are involved in a spiritual pilgrimage in which all help each other through personal sharing. They do not merely engage in discussion; they are in dialogue, and there is a difference. In mere discussion people may talk to each other without ever plumbing the depths. They will politely pass opinions, often without hearing others or without themselves being heard. In mere discussion there is not always real progress in understanding. The juice does not flow; but when discussion becomes dialogue the juice not only flows, it makes sugar. Sometimes it is bitter sugar, but it is substance, and progress is made in understanding.

Discussion can be dialogue, but dialogue is certainly much more than discussion. Lecture and dialogue are often said to be opposites, but the real opposites are lecture and discussion. Strange as it may seem even lecture can be dialogue, for dialogue is not so much a technique as it is an atmosphere or a relationship. True dialogue depends on one's ability to "cross over" to another's side of life. When Sunday School classrooms become dialogue, people find each other in love. Christ is made manifest, and souls are saved.

Kim was an Okinawan bride who had been reared in Shintoism and without the slightest glimmering of Christianity. Because she was lonely and without friends, she timidly accepted an invitation to join a young women's Bible study group. The language barrier was very great and she had difficulty understanding what was being said, but in that group there was something more important than words.

First, it was made up of lonely young women in search of understanding. They had become involved in the great personal chasms of life, and most had a sense of being lost at the bottom of their own private grand canyons. As they began to understand the Scriptures, they felt themselves upon a journey to close the distance between their private chasms.

Second, the members of the group saw one another as persons; and as they learned about Christ, they did not see each other as Okinawans, or Yankees, or Southerners but as persons. They lost their "tongue-tiedness" and began to live a true Christian fellowship without fear of losing anything from each other.

Third, they moved in mutual response to each other. They did not stop talking merely to decide what to say next, but to listen. They lived the spirit of Christ in loving respect for each other. Sometimes they talked, and sometimes they listened. They came to see that at times, in true dialogue, no talking is necessary.

Fourth, they had something vital to talk about. The Bible was open before them and the Word spoke to them out of its pages. The Word was Christ in their presence, and their acknowledgement of his presence became experience. Their mutual sharing of Christ and his love became a creative redemptive experience.

Kim found salvation, and became a different human being, not less Okinawan, but more human. She found in Christ a new solidarity with all mankind. Involvement together in exciting Bible study made a big difference in her life. This would not have happened in a nondynamic class, where the teacher talked more or less to himself and where the members left in a hurry as if escaping prison.

Studying the Bible in a Dynamic Manner

"How does one make Bible study dynamic?" you ask. Keeping in mind that dynamic Bible study derives from a basic dialogue situation in which the most important thing is attitude, not method, you still must give attention to method. As teacher you are largely responsible for method and should deliberately plan to secure the widest possible involvement of all the members. There are several simply but important things you can do.

1. Go to the class having clearly in mind what you hope to get done. Teaching a lesson without *teaching aims* is like driving a car without knowing your destination. The teaching aims in your quarterlies will help, but you will not always take these as they are written. You can rewrite them, or even substitute your own. The important thing is to know where you want to go in your teaching before you ever speak a single word.

2. Use a lesson plan in keeping with your aim. The football people have what they call "a game plan." Long before the first whistle blows they decide whether to play an offensive or a defensive game, and what to do as contingencies develop. Sometimes they scrap their plan, but they never fail to have it. Lesson plans should be designed to secure true dialogue, using whatever basic methods are appropriate. The teacher should know how to plan to open the lesson and how members are to be used in developing it. Rice Pierce suggests four basic classroom methods. (1) The informal discussion in which the lesson is informally discussed on the basis of planned questions. (2) The lecture-forum in which the teacher takes about fifteen minutes to present the facts and the rest of the time is spent in discussion. (3) The research forum which requires preclass assignments and small-group discussion. (4) The formal discussion which entails a series of preset steps. Developing a lesson plan requires the selection of one of these methods, but it also requires a careful organizing of your material.[2]

3. Tie your lesson to life. One favorite method is to carefully select a question which secures response of class members about something out of their experience. The question should be based on life experience, but should reflect the subject of the day. Throughout the lesson,

the teacher should ask other questions that will keep the contemporary in focus. The most exciting lessons are the ones that have direct bearing on the lives of the members.

4. Use props when appropriate, but don't substitute props for preparation. A gadget is never useful as an end within itself. For the ordinary classroom the two most useful props are blackboards and maps. Posters may also be used, as well as picture projectors, and felt boards. The way these are used is most important. Sometimes they actually interfere. Objects of various kinds are also helpful, but these should never be so prominent as to preempt the real class purpose.

5. Plan always for some discussion, no matter what your basic method. More learning takes place as people exchange ideas than when they are merely listening to a lecture. Some teachers do not like to use discussion because of "rabbit chasing" but I have seldom seen classes chase rabbits when the teacher really planned ahead of time for the discussion. If the teacher knows where he is going, the class will likely stay with him.

The Excitement of Seeing Others Learn

Sharing the Word with other people brings two different joys. One is the joy of expressing what one believes, not unlike the joy of performance or the joy of creativity. The other is the joy of watching the Word transform the lives of others. It is like seeing a rose bloom in the garden or a loaf of bread rising in the oven. The way a successful and caring teacher gets involved in the lives of his students is unlike any other professional person. In ordinary teaching it is as though the teacher sees himself unfolding in his students; in Bible teaching it is as though the teacher sees Christ coming alive in his students. There is true excitement in this, not like one sees at a circus or in the ice follies, or one experiences when one's favorite football team wins the crucial game in the last two minutes. Rather, it is the quiet excitement that sustains life and interest, and that makes the rainiest day a happy day, the lasting excitement that prolongs the vitality and the years of the teacher.

Sharing the Word Is to See Understanding Develop

Some people understand the Bible when they first hear it read or read it for themselves, but most do not. They are like the Ethiopian eunuch Philip found reading the Scriptures in the chariot. Philip asked him, "Understandest thou what thou readest?" The eunuch replied, "How can I, except some man should guide me?" (Acts 8:30–31). Most people need careful guidance in understanding the Word of God. When guidance is not present, and where men rely only on their own understanding, the result may be a Muhammad who distorts the Scripture into Islam, or a Joseph Smith who distorts it into Mormonism, or a Mary Baker Eddy who distorts it into Christian Science.

Most people must begin in their study of the Word "as newborn babes" (1 Pet. 2:2). They must be taught to "desire the sincere milk of the word." Paul said to the Corinthians: "I have fed you with milk, and not with meat: for hitherto ye were not able to bear it, neither yet now are ye able" (1 Cor. 3:2). Knowing what is the milk of the Scriptures and what is the meat and when to administer each requires teachers of great skill and patience.

The highest reward a teacher can have is suddenly to see understanding break out on the face of the pupil. The whole expression changes and the happy words are heard, "I see." As the truth of God's Word is understood, it is as if the pupil says, "I see and am changed."

Sharing the Word of God Is to See Fellowship Come Alive

My mother was a member of a T.E.L. Sunday School class for nearly fifty years. She joined it as a young woman and faithfully studied the Bible under the leadership of a half-dozen strong, caring teachers. The solidarity of that class was quite remarkable. It was a true Christian fellowship that helped the members through the sorrows of loss of fortune, of children, and of husbands. Her life would have been most barren without its love and support.

The strength of the class was that at its center was the Word of God. Its members studied the Bible and lived by the Bible. They lived long enough in that fellowship for it to make a real difference in their lives and characters. In our day mobility has taken its toll, and many of us are never in one place long enough to taste the deep fellowship of those who have lived with the Bible and with each other through extended periods of happiness and sorrow. Yet strangely, even with our great moving about, the Word of God draws even strangers together in loving, creative, exciting fellowship.

People who sincerely learn the Scriptures develop a concern for both the Lord and other Christians. There is a direct relationship between Bible study and the vitality of a congregation. Paul said, "Let the word of Christ dwell in you richly in all wisdom; teaching and admonishing one another in psalms and hymns and spiritual songs, singing with grace in your hearts to the Lord" (Col. 3:16).

Sharing the Word of God Is to See Souls Saved

One of the spiritual tragedies of our times is the lack of understanding and acceptance of the New Testament idea of lostness. Modern man does not see himself as lost and needing a Savior. If you don't believe this, then tune in on the average man's thinking as he sees roadside signs that say, "Prepare to meet thy God," or, "Jesus saves." He is such a pragmatist that he admits no alienation whatever from God or from eternity. He dismisses any appeal to him to face his lostness as outmoded nonsense, and he even assaults those confronting him as evil because as he would put it, "They are trying to make me feel guilty." He does not believe in hell, or that "the wages of sin is death." Simply telling him he is lost is like honking at a traffic signal. He goes on flashing his little light completely indifferent to all appeals.

Yet the man is lost, and he can be made to feel it, not by admonition or exhortation but by an honest confrontation of the Scriptures. The Bible speaks plainly on this subject. Jesus said, "Ye do err, not knowing the scriptures, nor the power of God" (Matt. 22:29). "It is the spirit [of God] that quickeneth . . . the words I speak unto you, they are spirit, and they are life" (John 6:63). Paul said, "Faith cometh by hearing, and hearing by the word of God" (Rom. 10:17). "When ye received the word of God . . . ye received it not as the word of men, but as it is in truth, the word of God, which effectually worketh also in you that believe" (1 Thess. 2:13). James said, "Of his own will begat he us with the word of truth, that we should be a kind of firstfruit of his creatures" (Jas. 1:18).

The Word of God can do more to arouse in men their sense of lostness than anything else we can do or say. The Holy Spirit uses it to convict and to save. Teachers who Sunday after Sunday share the Word of God soon see miracles take place in the lives of timid lost souls who slowly begin to understand their lostness and find in Christ the answer to their desperation. What could be more exciting?

Sharing the Word of God Is to See the Church Grow

The church that grows is one that honors the Word of God and sees it as a rich treasure to share with the whole world. If it becomes preoccupied with other types of ministry to the exclusion of the basic teaching of the Bible and the straightforward presentation of Christ, it surrenders its uniqueness as a spiritual institution.

When Peter and John were confronted by the lame man in Solomon's Gate of the Temple and heard his plea for alms, they faced several options: (1) They could have reached into their pockets and given him the coins he begged. (2) They could have directed him to the office for the employment of the handicapped. (3) They could have sent him to a psychiatrist. (4) Or they could have put him into a program for the rehabilitation of the physically disabled. So caught up were they in the words of God that none of these options occurred to them. Instead Peter said, "Silver and gold have I none; but such as I have, give I thee: In the name of Jesus Christ of Nazareth rise up and walk" (Acts 3:6).

The church has no option in its basic work of confronting the whole world for Christ. It grows only as it does this work, and its basic tool for doing it is the Word of God. Hospitalization, psychiatry, programs for the handicapped, and other similar things are acceptable vehicles for the gospel, but only as ways the church lives out the spirit of Christ. They are not ways of salvation. Only Christ can save, and the way men are brought face to face with him is through the Scriptures.

So many churches, though claiming to give first place to the teaching of the Word of God, tend to let other things get in the way. One congregation organized a study group to determine its purpose and what it ought to be doing about it. The study group concluded that the Bible was obsolete, and in its place recommended study of the great social issues of the times. The final outcome cannot be anything but disastrous, for apart from the Word of God, the church has no mandate, no inspiration, no method, and no power.

Only two of the larger non-Catholic American denominations report advancement during the last few years: Missouri Synod Lutherans and Southern Baptists. Both of these denominations make the Bible central in their teaching and preaching; both are unapologetically conservative; both make uncompromising demands on their members; both are fervently evangelical; and both have strong programs of religious education in which the Bible is the textbook. No wonder there is growth and excitement in their churches.

At the beginning of this chapter, there were enumerated twelve reasons for dull Sunday morning Bible study. Things do not have to be that way in your church. They can be different if these reasons are turned around and used as a positive ladder for bringing new life to your Bible study:

(1) Accept the premise that the Bible is a "now" book, and that it has as much relevance to contemporary life as it did in the day it was written.

(2) Recognize the Holy Spirit in your presence and believe with all your heart that he will bless your teaching.

(3) Make plenty of room for informality in your Bible discussions. Try to escape the speaker-audience syndrome.

(4) Make room for dialogue, remembering that it is more than conversation and discussion.

(5) Avoid all deadly set routines in class study.

(6) Try to create some Bible study situations in which the ages are mixed, youth and adults for example.

(7) Build fellowship into your building and your routines with wider halls, more conversational areas, and more flexible schedules.

(8) Use the most modern communication methods in getting our message out to the world.

(9) Become more positive and more emphatic in your teaching, while avoiding harshness and defensiveness.

(10) Try enthusiasm both in your planning and in your preparation.

(11) Do not apologize for your separation from the world. Accept gracefully the strictness of the Christian tradition.

(12) Use your imagination in presenting Bible study and in expending Bible study opportunities.

4] [Personal Word Bearing

On the island of Borneo in Indonesia there is a man and wife who have spent their lives in "the ministry of the Word." They are not teachers and they do not pastor churches, yet thousands remember them as spiritual parents. They travel for weeks in a Volkswagen bus fitted with cots for sleeping and with shelves for books and pamphlets.

Most of what they sell are copies of the Bible, sometimes in its whole form, but more often in Scripture portions. When their stock runs low, they return to their tiny apartment for rest and to fill their shelves for another trip, this time in a different direction and to a different language, for Indonesia is a vast country that speaks many tongues. Nothing but the call of God could keep them going year after year in such hard work in this strange and sometimes unfriendly land. Their lives are a mission, not for the sake of mission but for the sake of Christ. They are held by deep Christian commitment, and though they realize that some Christians are not sympathetic they serve valiantly and without complaint.

A missionary from India after preaching in an English church told James Denney: "I have been pouring out my life in India, and I have come home to find that people who are supposed to support us don't care. I don't think they believe in missions." To which Denney replied, "They have no right to believe in missions, for they do not believe in Jesus Christ."

Eagerness to share always walks hand in hand with the willingness to believe. A decline in evangelism follows a decline in faith. P. T. Forsyth said, "You may always measure the value of Christ's cross by your interest in missions. The missionless church betrays a crossless church, and it becomes a faithless church."

If the judgments of Denney and Forsyth seem extreme, then consider that of Dr. Samuel Shoemaker, an American pastor in the Episcopal church: "I am shocked to find how many people in our churches have never made a decisive Christian commitment. They oozed into church membership on a conventional kind of basis but no one has ever effectively dealt with them spiritually, or helped them make a Christian decision."

Oozing into church membership does not create fervent dedication. Such people cannot be counted to support the mission program of the church, much less become personal ministers of the word of God.

The moment one submits to Christian discipline, he accepts the obligation to join in helping make all men see the unsearchable riches of Christ. He becomes a member of what Tom Allen calls "the overwhelming minority." Gideon's tiny hand, the twelve disciples, the 120 in the upper room, and Paul's itinerant mission group—these symbolize the dynamic power of God's overwhelming minority. Like the tiny village of Plymouth in 1621, the overwhelming minority stands precariously at the edge of a vast spiritual wilderness. It exists for others, not for itself. The church is, apparently, the only organization in the world that performs its work wholly for others. Its work, of course, is its mission for Christ, and it never really accomplishes its work until all of its members become personal Word-bearers to the world.

In its ministry of the Word, the church must work two ways. As a whole, every member helps every other member in the task of preaching and teaching. As individuals, members are in day-to-day contact with other people in the world. True Christians are not mere spectators but participants. Elton Trueblood says they are unlike the orchestra society who hires the orchestra and listens to the music but like the orchestra itself. They are the musicians, and they make the music. Sometimes they play in unison, more often they play their own parts at the same time, and when they leave the orchestra hall they play solos.

An orchestra can become so involved in the study of music that it forgets to play, and a church involved in worship and service can forget that it exists for missions. George Sweazey said, "A church always tends to drift away from evangelism, never toward it." There must be a deliberate burning and scattering of the fire of God if the church is to do its work in the world. The burning is done as the church worships and teaches its members, and the scattering is done as the members become Word-bearers to the world.

Living the Word for All the World to See

For one to become an effective Word-bearer unto the world, he must receive the Word into his own life, letting it saturate his soul until it totally conditions his consciousness. He must truly learn how to live the Scriptures. Learning and living the Scriptures is more than learning about God or being informed about Christ or knowing moral laws. It is to know God, to be transformed by Christ, and to be endued with power to put moral laws into effect. It is to totally absorb the impact of the Bible, so that its word becomes the Word of God for you, and its wisdom, the Wisdom of God for your life. When David said, "I have laid up thy word in my heart, that I might not sin against thee" (Ps. 119:11, RSV), he was putting into a single sentence one of the points of the vast doctrine of God's communication. In a sense the Scriptures are God's personal telephone cables into the heart and will of man. They are always there, and they come alive when God begins to speak to him through them.

Faithfulness in Reading God's Word

A young man contracted with a large Bible-publishing firm to sell Bibles door-to-door in Northern Ohio. After a successful summer, he was asked to return the next year in a supervisory position, but he immediately declined. He told his father, "I could not go on selling expensive Bibles to people who never read them, and who obviously bought them out of superstition. I don't want to capitalize on this kind of abuse of the Bible."

There are millions who take God's book superstitiously, like those who display statues of saints in their cars to ward off traffic accidents. Are you one of them? Do you have a finely-bound and printed copy on your coffee table or your desk, its pages brittle with unuse? Do you use it as a place to hide money and press flowers? Do you pick it up only to record the birth dates of your children and other anniversaries? Do you have to dust it off when you know the minister is coming?

Reading the Bible every day keeps your heart open to God's speaking to you. Samuel Taylor Coleridge once said, "In the Bible there is more that finds me than I have experienced in all other books put together; the morals of the Bible find me at greater depths of my being; and whatever finds me brings with it an irresistible evidence of its having preceded from the Holy Spirit."

Reading the Bible builds the church. Yes, it is that simple: reading the Bible builds the church. A. M. Chirgwin in *The Bible in World Evangelism* tells of a group in rural Spain who read the Scriptures. A working girl rescued a gospel portion from a small stream where someone had discarded it. "Out of curiosity she rescued it, took it home, dried it and later *read* it. It was a copy of St. John's Gospel. She *read* it a second time; then she *read* it to her family; and after that she *read* it to her neighbors. Gradually a little group formed a habit of coming on Sundays to hear it *read*. In due time they built a place for their meetings and formed themselves into an evangelical church." [1]

Reading the Bible prepares the Christian to witness to the world. It tells others that he takes his commitment seriously. Two men traveled together for a month; one was a Christian, the other was not. The Christian did not know he was being closely observed by the other to see if he was genuinely committed to his cause.

At the journey's end he attempted to witness to his unsaved friend and much to his surprise received a blunt reply: "No, I will have to think about it quite a while longer, for I am not sure you are really committed to the Christian way. Not once have I seen you read the Bible. You've eagerly studied travel folders to find out about the sights we were to see and you've read the newspapers to learn about the world we live in, but I've not seen you turn to the Bible to learn God's thoughts for you." If one ever hopes to become an effective personal minister of the Word, he must remove even the slightest doubt about his daily loyalty to Bible study.

Reading the Bible enables one to be more articulate in expressing his faith to others. Telling others is difficult for most people to learn. They are tongue-tied and timid, partly because of a natural reluctance to talk about personal spiritual experiences, but mostly because of an oral unfamiliarity with the words and pictures of the New Testament. They know them well enough as listeners, but scarcely at all as speakers, a deficit that intensive daily study of the Bible will correct. The denominations that greatly emphasize Bible study seem to develop more aggressive and personal evangelists. One of them is the Churches of Christ, long noted for Sunday morning and evening Bible studies. People trained under their leadership have no reticence and no lack of skill in personal aggressive evangelism. Could it be that constant use of the Bible is responsible for this?

Faithfulness Is Listening to God's Voice Through His Word

Reading the Scripture is like looking at a sunrise in an Arizona sky. Viewing it as a physicist, one sees the earth turning toward the sun with dust and moisture in the air to give an illusion of color. Viewing it as an artist, one sees it as reds and yellows and blues and greens fused into exciting variations of patterns and shades from the mingling of the burning rays of the fiery sun. To the physicist the sunrise is a fact of nature, to the artist an experience. The artist looks at the sunrise expecting to see something more and better than the turning of the earth toward the sun.

One who reads the Bible should look for much more than the words on the pages. He should learn to listen with the heart to what too often escapes those who see only the words. Augustus H. Strong said, "Christ has not so constructed Scripture as to dispense presence and teaching by his Spirit." The Bible is called "the sword of the Spirit" (Eph. 6:17). Unless the Spirit uses it as his own rapier to penetrate the soul, it will never truly enter the human life. Again as Strong said, "Only the Holy Spirit can turn the outer word into the inner word. . . . He bears testimony to Scripture even more than the Scripture bears testimony to him."

The Christian who really wants to become a Word-bearer to the world must let himself be swept off his feet by the sunrise of God's presence in his book. He must listen as God imparts his own consciousness into man and sets him on the road to witness.

At first as one listens to the Spirit speaking through the Word, he hears only diversity—forty writers including shepherds, fishermen, priests, soldiers, statesmen, tax collectors, and philosophers writing over a period of over a thousand years. Yet as one continues to listen he hears unity, for those men produced a book of unparalleled spiritual and moral integrity. The singleness of purpose is seen in the saying of Jesus: "Think not that I am come to destroy the law, or the prophets: I came not to destroy, but to fulfil" (Matt. 5:17).

60

All through this vast unity the believer senses God is seeking to enter the consciousness of man. As he reads the Bible, he begins to feel that whoever inspired it also made him. As he openly surrenders to its truth, he is drawn into God's love and becomes himself a creation of the Word. A blending of God's consciousness with his consciousness takes place without God downgrading himself or robbing the believer of his freedom. It is as though another mind is taking shape in man. The blending force is Jesus Christ, also called the Word. Paul said, "I am crucified with Christ: nevertheless I live" (Gal. 2:20). Through Christ, God lives in the believer and energizes him for righteousness; yet he still keeps his dignity and his freedom and continues to grow as a human being.

The milieu of this transfer is the written Word presenting the personal Word. As the word of life, we listen to it; as the water of life, we drink it; as the bread of life we eat it; as the power of life, we surrender to it. And at the end of all of our eating and drinking and listening and surrender, we discover the mind of Christ and thus come to live with the consciousness of God.

Listening to the Word of God draws the Christian into the fellowship of the concerned. Peter, James, and John were carried to the mount of transfiguration and later to the garden of Gethsemane, into an intimate circle which did not include the other disciples, probably because they listened a little more carefully to what Jesus did and said. They were always nearest at hand when Jesus had some need or faced some crisis. Only the women lingered closer during the tragic hours of the cross. Among Christians there always seems to be a group more dependable in the church than others. Usually these are people who have learned to listen deeply to God's Word speaking to them in the Bible and from the pulpit. They are part of the fellowship of the concerned. They are Sunday-night and Wednesday-night Christians.

Speaking the Word of God for All the World to Hear

G. M. Chirgwin tells of a Brazillian colporteur who had a unique method of distribuiting the Scriptures to commuters riding trains out of Rio de Janeiro. Just as the noise of the train stopped, he would shout from one end of the coach, something like this: "This book tells you everything you need to know." Then he would walk down the aisle calling out Bible verses as headlines, selling his Scripture portions. At the next station he would work another car. By the end of the trip he would have sold all his books.

Another train rider in New York City spends his evening on the subways. When the train stops, he calls out a Bible verse through his battered megaphone. When asked why he is doing this, he said: "God has called me to shout the Scriptures on the subway."

A retired carpenter living in Nashville, Tennessee, traveled back and forth to Florida using different routes. On the way he would erect small signs on which he had printed verses of Scripture. At the end of the journey he would make more signs to erect on the way home.

Bill Glass, a professional football player felt God's call to preach the gospel. When his career ended, he entered the seminary. Today he is a highly successful evangelist. From one end of the nation to another he preaches God's Word to thousands of youth as they crowd the halls to hear him.

Billy Graham began his evangelistic ministry more than thirty years ago. He has reached millions and today is problably the best-known American. Over and over in his sermons on radio and TV, he speaks without apology, "The Bible says."

A young man with a brilliant mind surrendered his life to teach in the seminary. He earned two doctor's degrees and became highly proficient in the ancient biblical language. A scholar in every sense of the word, he has left his imprint on thousands of young people.

Von Worten is an Oklahoman who left the broad prairies of his native state to give himself to the rural areas of Java. He works in isolated villages, sometimes preaching as many as five sermons a day. Wherever he goes he takes copies of the New Testament to sell for a few pennies. He may not have the audiences of Bill Glass and Billy Graham, but he is just as faithful as they are in personal Word bearing. He speaks plainly and boldly the Word of God to the world.

A retired dentist in a Florida resort gathers with other Christians on Thursday night for church visitation. Armed with Scripture portions he drives out into the community to confront people for Christ in a most winsome and convincing way. He leaves a marked Scripture portion for later reading. His life has touched thousands.

These men are not hired announcers to speak first one thing and then another. They are committed men who have laid their lives on the line to speak for Christ. They speak because they have chosen to speak.

Speaking the Word of God in Your Life Choices

When Ernest Hemingway began to write novels, filled as they were with profanity, sex, and violence, the people in his hometown who had known him as a young man were shocked. Some of them said, "This is not our Ernest, the high-minded young man we once knew." The truth is that long before he revealed himself publicly in print Ernest had committed himself to a profligate life. His choices finally led to a suicide's grave.

Some psychologists write about the controlling influence of the "self-image." The image one carries of himself has much to do with his mental health and his life performance. Some of them say that one reason for a person's poor self-image is guilt. These observations seem to agree in some ways with the New Testament. Judas smote his breast out of remorse for his betrayal of Christ, a perfect model of a man with a poor self-image. Peter, retreating in shame on a fishing trip, was brought face-to-face by the Lord with a rotten self-image he was trying to hide.

Surely Jesus means for all men to think well of themselves else he would not have said, "Love thy neighbour as thyself" (Matt. 19:19). He frequently reminded men of their sins—not to create guilt as some hold—but to face them and to be rid of them. As long as guilt stays unfaced and unrepented, it remains an impossible weight to bear and it creates a damning self-image. Life turns stringy and sour. When Jesus said to the lame man at the pool of Bethesda, "Sin no more" (John 5:14), he was asking him to shed his guilt and begin again by taking a new good self-image.

The choice makes the difference. Either one chooses his own poor self-image that he cannot abide and which could lead him to a suicide grave; or, he chooses the good image Christ has of him as being someone who is worthwhile. The Bible helps him make the choice. The more one absorbs the Scriptures, the easier are his moral and spiritual choices. When he chooses, he becomes his choice. Choosing his inferior self-image he becomes even more guilty; choosing his image in Christ, he becomes more Christlike.

63

It was sometimes said of General Douglas MacArthur that even in civilian clothing he looked like a soldier. His life choices were reflected in his character. It is the same with Christians, as they choose, they will speak for God.

Speaking Through the Life We Live

> There's something I've often heard,
> A deed outshouts the word;
> But yet with spiritual need
> The Word outshouts the deed.

Behind every great verbal testimony of God's goodness there stands a greater deed of God's action. John wrote in the Revelation, "They overcame him by the blood of the Lamb, and by the word of their testimony" (Rev. 12:11). The great action is the cross, and the preaching is the word of testimony. God's action always precedes man's preaching. The spoken word is nothing without the deed behind it, but with the deed behind it, the word becomes the Word. The deed validates and energizes the word.

It is the same with man, for unless there is a cross in his life, his speaking is in vain. He must live before he preaches. Paul said, "Though I speak with the tongues of men and of angels, and have not charity [love], I am become as sounding brass and tinkling cymbals" (1 Cor. 13:1). A word without a cross is pretentious and unsatisfying. True, then it is that the deed outshouts the word. If there is no deed, it nullifies the Word; if there is a wrong deed, it discredits the Word, but if there is the deed of love it expands and heightens the Word and makes it music to the sinner's ear.

Jesus makes it plain that the good life is the only life that can speak for him. He said, "Be ye therefore perfect, even as your Father which is in heaven is perfect" (Matt. 5:48). It is also written, "Follow peace with all men, and holiness, without which no man shall see the Lord" (Heb. 12:14). He knows these ideals are unattainable, yet he urges man to seek perfection in him, and to let him make of them what he will. The Bible itself is one of the means by which man understands his union with Christ. In its pages we see that the Christian faith is a faith of relationships. We learn that man must have a good relation both with God and with his neighbor. Attaining these, man has both the right and the power for witness.

Attainment must be on God's terms. One cannot follow both God and self, and he cannot love God and mammon. To try is to be divided within and to totally discredit one's witness for righteousness. His life lacks integrity. He is not a whole person. Only as he throws off mammon and wholly serves God can he be an authentic witness. Moreover, God requires man to be at peace with his neighbor. If he is a prima donna among men, insensitive in his listening to others, unheeding in his contacts with others, unserving the needs of others, and if he does not move among people as a peacemaker, he not only fails to build up life; he actually destroys it. If he tries to speak God's word to the world, the people will not only reject his message, they will despise him.

Thomas A. Harris in his book *I'm OK, You're OK* brilliantly describes three types of attitude at work inside grown men. One he calls "the child" which speaks selfishly, irresponsibly in tones, often irrationally and emotionally. Another he calls "the parent" who speaks possessively and with unexamined "shoulds." The third is "the adult" who speaks reasonably and hopefully. These three compete with each other and as they win they shape the personalities. The book is a most satisfying interpretation of human nature and should be read by everyone, remembering that the idea is not really new.

Paul discussed it at length in Romans 7 and he alluded to it in such passages as "When I was a child I spake as a child . . . but when I became a man, I put away childish things" (i Cor. 13:11). Harris' idea is that we cannot become authentic, natural, and free personalities until we put ourselves under the control of the adult within us. Paul goes one step further, we cannot be authentic, natural, and free personalities until we put ourselves under control of the Christ within us. Living the spirit of Christ, having the mind of Christ, reflecting his life, following his law—this becomes for the Christian a life-style which can compel others to listen to him when he speaks of God's Word. Yes, first it is the deed that outshouts the Word, and then the Word that outshouts the deed.

Speaking Through the Words We Say

Men who live in monasteries where human speech is not used are as guilty of the abuse of personality as the ancient Chinese who bound the feet of little girls. The complex mechanisms of human speech and hearing are gifts from God, and are meant to be used often and well. The old cliche that one picture is worth ten thousand words is an overworked exaggeration. Pictures indeed have their places and they do indeed sometimes say things that words cannot say. Yet would pictures have any meaning at all without the words that preceded them? In a way words are pictures.

When words are spoken, they become so much more meaningful with the use of inflections and stresses, and they carry an infinite variety of emotions. Scientists in taking electronic pictures of the human voice have discovered that no two people talk alike. Voice prints are as different as fingerprints. Surely God has purpose for all this variety. Every person has his own unique contribution to make.

Every Christian therefore should speak up for Christ; he should utter his word of faith in public, because when the world hears from him, it hears a facet of the gospel never heard before, and perhaps never to be heard again. Surely the unerring hand of God has placed him here to speak now, in their place, in his own manner of speaking, to those people who may never hear the gospel except as he speaks it. No matter how weak he feels, or how slow his speech, he still must speak and be a Word bearer for the Lord.

As you have read, you probably have thought that "Well, this all is about evangelism." Yes, it is indeed all about evangelism, if you understand all of life as evangelistic and everything you do as outreach for Christ. No, if you think that this is all there is to evangelism and you think you can escape direct witness bearing with the idea of bringing people through Christ to walk with God. In a sense the discussion thus far in this chapter is preevangelism. Now it is time to speak of the Word bearer as evangelist.

Pressing the Word for All the World to Hear

Long before evangelism becomes a program, it must be a passion. If not, then all activity and organization is in vain. Indeed, one serious obstruction to present-day evangelism is that it is seen by some as only a method or technique. Do these three things in this order and this man will surrender to Christ! Take these ten steps and you will have a great revival! Surely, the things to be done and the steps

66

to be taken are important, for there is a right and a wrong way to do anything; yet the work is nothing unless it is accompanied with the power of passion. Evangelism is born out of the heart that cares.

Pinpointing the sources of power for Christian witness is not always an easy task. Sometimes it appears to grow out of love, other times out of Bible study, and others from a walk with the Holy Spirit. As a matter of fact, it is from all three and many other sources besides. Probably the real source of power is the Holy Spirit; yet he yields himself only to love and to a knowledge of the Word. If the Holy Spirit is the spring of power, then the Bible is the map that leads us to the spring and the teacher that shows us how to drink from it.

All great witnesses from Christ have two things in common: (1) They have intimate knowledge of the Bible and (2) they know how to use the Bible in witnessing to others. Luke said of the eloquent Apollos that he was "mighty in the scriptures" (Acts 18:24) and that "he mightily convinced the Jews . . . publicly, showing by the scriptures that Jesus was Christ" (v. 28).

Studying the Scriptures, one senses that there is a great urgency in evangelism. The Bible is very clear in its teaching of the lostness of man, a reality that not many people want to admit or to face today. Sometimes we wonder why they are so hesitant. Perhaps it is because suddenly the world is so crowded that the average person never spends time alone in prolonged separation from others. The modern consciousness does not include much sense of lostness like being abandoned alone in the woods, or in the dark, or on a mountain. It is easy to assume that because we are always in touch with people, we are never lost. It is also easy to assume that since man does not know physical lostness, there is no such thing as spiritual lostness. It is to dispel this illusion that the Bible speaks over and over again.

Still modern man rejects his own lostness. A lawyer chiding a minister asked: "What do you mean by the heavy weight of sin? How much does it weigh? Ten pounds? Thirty pounds? A hundred pounds?" A frivolous and irresponsible universalism has led many to assume that all men everywhere are saved regardless of their choices or their sins. To take this view is to totally disregard the Bible and its teachings on the nature of sin and guilt and man's freedom of will.

Also it is to take a limited view of men as belonging only to the place where he is and the time that he lives.

God's view is quite different. Man is a cosmic creature; he belongs to all places and to all time. He cannot escape the fact that he must live also in eternity. If he stops to think about himself, surely he will see himself as infinitely small and infinitely lost among all the stars and galaxies of the universe and all the reaches of time. He must live and grow amidst a vast cosmic environment which he cannot understand but which he must master. Amidst all of this, he may not be lost from his neighbor, but he is surely lost from God.

The more man knows of his universe, the smaller he becomes. Every new insight into the human mind reveals it as unfathomable; every new piece of knowledge reveals knowledge as unending and every new surge of emotion reveals a depthless chasm of uncontrollable impulse. No wonder the psalmist prayed, "What is man that thou art mindful of him?" (Heb. 2:6). Modern man, completely out of control of himself, a pygmy in his own environment, is more lost than he has ever been; yet he does not know it.

Our greatest opportunity for Christ will come when all of man's empty panaceas are blown away and he begins to knock on the door of heaven for his needs. He does not yet knock, for he does not yet fully know his plight. He does not realize that he daily builds with his sin and his pride the very hell he so vehemently denies. The law of God still stands, "The wages of sin is death" (Rom. 6:23). "Be not deceived; God is not mocked; for whatsoever a man soweth, that shall he also reap" (Gal. 6:7). All the sowing to the flesh—narcotics, dishonor for parents, neglect of the family, disregard of the wisdom of the race, abandonment of opportunity for the development of God-given talents, abuse of little children, violation of marriage laws, illicit sex, eating bread without earning it—all of this is overwhelming lostness. God's awful warning is inescapable. "He who sows to his own flesh will from the flesh reap corruption."

Soon, very soon, America must awaken to the lostness of its sons and daughters. If it does, an awakening greater than the two Great Awakenings of the eighteenth and nineteenth centuries put together will take place. If it does not, then God's judgment will fall against us. We will reap the corruption of the spirit from the corruption of the flesh, and all will be lost.

The only tenable position for the Christian is to press the Word of God into all human hearts everywhere. "The seed is the word" and "the field is the world" (Luke 8:11; Matt. 13:38). Evangelism is not an occasional probing by a small scouting force; it is a continuing battle by all the people of God to all corners of the earth. It is the storming of the last stronghold. Years ago an Oklahoma evangelist was noted both for his preaching and for his personal work. During revivals, the afternoons would find him going with the pastor from home to home where he would read the Bible and explain its meaning. After returning from one long walk through a dusty field where he had read the Scriptures to a farmer still sitting on his tractor, the evangelist said: "Pressing the battle to the gates, that's what we are doing and it is so important."

Pressing from the Authority of Experience

Samuel Shoemaker in his book *How to Become a Christian* said, "The test of a man's conversion is whether he has enough Christianity to get it over to other people. If he hasn't there is something wrong with it." This frank statement is a coin with two sides: (1) One must have had a true experience with Christ in order to successfully share him, and (2) if one has had a true experience he will share it.

This famous Episcopalian evangelist floundered about in his ministry until one day in Peking, China, a man challenged him as to whether or not he had made a full commitment to Christ, and held him mercilessly to the challenge until he was done in. The next day he was able to lead a young Chinese businessman to Christ. Shoemaker also wrote: "Test yourself by this: Can I get across to other people what I believe about Jesus Christ? If not, what good am I to them, and what good am I to him?"

Old-time ministers used to have a way of saying that soul-winning is one beggar telling another beggar where to find bread. The point is that a man who has experienced hunger knows where to find food, and how to tell another man quickly where to find it. There is no substitute for experience in talking to others about Jesus.

The apostle Paul's conversion turned him completely around from a narrow, vindicative Pharisaism to a broad Christian spirit. Frequently, he used his experience both as motivation and as example in his witness to other people. The word of Paul's testimony itself

69

became Scripture. Take away his experience and you remove the keystone of all his writing and speaking. Paul was able to convince others because he had seen for himself. The Christian experience is something that must be told.

> I went into a prayer place,
>   And heard an inner call.
> I bowed my head in simple faith,
>   And entered heaven's hall.
>
> I dreamed of wrong's destructive snare,
>   Of all that might have been.
> I saw my life in wasted blight,
>   Had I not Jesus seen?
>
> So now I must retell once more
>   The glory of the light
> That came by simple Christian faith
>   To snatch my life from night.

One does not quickly and easily learn to share his experience, but if he has had an authentic meeting with the Lord, he can learn. Two things can help. One is a daily walk with the Bible. It is surprising how much one learns about witnessing by studying the New Testament. The other is to participate in one of the lay witnessing schools sponsored by your denomination. To learn how to witness is to become a part of an overcoming life.

Samuel Shoemaker discusses the power of the spoken word. He says: "The word of personal witness to Christ on the part of one who knows Him may beget faith in someone else who has never been touched in any other way. Not long ago I met a man who has lived for the things of this world almost wholly. No one ever moved him till he met a layman who lives in his part of the country, who was once a pagan himself, but now lives by the power of Christ. The joy and contagion, the unselfishness and optimism, the fearless courage to speak naturally and humanly about his Lord, touched this man's heart. 'He is the best Christian I ever met,' he said. That kind of speaking which arises out of living and moves from one life to another is one of the great channels of spiritual power. We need millions more Christians who learn how to do it." [2]

Pressing with Words That Penetrate

In his book *The Company of the Committed,* Elton Trueblood suggests that most of the figures of speech that Jesus used to symbolize the gospel—salt, light, keys, bread, water, leaven, fire—all have a single thing in common: penetration.

Trueblood says, "The purpose of the salt is to penetrate the meat and thus preserve it; the function of light is to penetrate the darkness; the only use of a key is to penetrate the lock; bread is worthless until it penetrates the body; water penetrates the hard crust of earth; leaven the dough to make it rise; fire continues only as it reaches new fuel and the best way to extinguish it is to contain it." [3]

This graphic picture by Trueblood emphasizes the adaptability of the Word of God to every condition of the human heart and mind. It also marks the power of the Scripture to enter the human heart where the mere words of man cannot enter. "All scripture is given by inspiration of God, and is profitable for doctrine, for reproof, for correction, for instruction in righteousness: that the man of God may be perfect, thoroughly furnished unto all good works" (2 Tim. 3: 16–17). Somehow we must restore America's confidence in the efficacy of God's Word. We must convince church leaders that it is God's Word for all men everywhere and all the time, or it is not God's Word for any man, anywhere, anytime! They must be taught to press it home to every man.

The word "Word" appears in reference to the gospel dozens of times, and every time with a new facet. The "word" is

the word with signs (Mark 16:20)
the word of exhortation (Acts 13:15)
the word of salvation (Acts 13:26)
the word of his grace (Acts 20:32)
the word of faith (Rom. 10:8)
the word of wisdom (1 Cor. 12:8)
the word without fear (Phil. 1:14)
the word of life (Phil. 2:16)
the word of the truth (Col. 1:5)

the word instant (2 Tim. 4:2)
the word of power (Heb. 1:3)
the word of righteousness (Heb. 5:13)
the word of exhortation (Heb. 13:22)
the word of prophecy (2 Pet. 1:9)
the word of patience (Rev. 3:10)
the word of testimony (Rev. 12:11)
the word abiding (John 5:38)
the word not passing away (Matt. 24:35)

The "sword of the Spirit" is a sword of many edges. As diverse as human life is, there is always some facet of the Word that the Holy Spirit can use to convict and to call. It penetrates to the marrow of the soul; so let us press it without apology.

Pressing the Word Specifically

Church people have retreated into preaching a kind of "to whom it may concern Christianity." The hour for such timidity is past. The time always comes when one must leave the study and go to the pulpit, then leave the pulpit and go to the people, then leave people and go to a person, then leave generalities and confront the specific person in terms of his own life and future. It is in this outreach for the lost person that our evangelistic zeal is tested. Many a man has hesitated just before knocking on the door, only to turn away and walk around the block praying fervently for help. He goes back to the door a stronger man. It is tough to deal personally with a man on a subject as sensitive as his soul; yet it is the thing we are called to do, and to do well.

Many a soul-winner has stumbled through his testimony, only later to reexamine it and to rephrase it, to emerge a stronger and more effective Christian. Translating one's theology into practical words for interpretation to the unsaved strengthens one's faith, and prepares one for the tough opposition he is sure to encounter along the way.

People appear to resist the pleas of friends who talk to them about Christ. This is because they carry deep conviction of something wrong in their lives, criticizing both churches and Christians, mostly out of fear of their own guilt. It takes special courage and training to deal with them. Most conservative denominations have developed lay witness training institutes to help men and women acquire skills for the task. One of the most thorough is offered by the evangelism leaders of the Southern Baptist Convention.

Personal Word bearing, this marks the truly committed Christian. It does not mean we must quote Bible verses to fit every occasion or that we must make ourselves unbearable in speaking the Word. Indeed we have an obligation to speak carefully and winsomely when we speak to the gospel. Ours is a community of joy, and the joy should be seen by the world. We are not dooms-dayers and crepe-hangers, but people of redemption and people of hope. It is our obligation to let people see the friendship of Christ. As Word bearers we must press the battle to the gates, speaking the joy of Christ and creating a fellowship that will swallow up all the evils of the world.

5] [The Church Sharing by Extending

We walked the black sands of the Java beach and felt night falling quickly over the quiet sea. The sun was no more than a fading shadow of red light against the blue-gray sky. Behind we heard the hollow sound of wood against wood. "They are threshing rice. Would you like to see it?" someone asked. A few minutes later we stood under a huge arbor built of bamboo poles and rice straw, and we watched three tiny Javanese women with heavy poles beat a cadent song to the gods, using the threshing trough as a drum. Then prompted by a hidden signal they began pounding a ten-pound sheath of rice, holding the straw with their bare feet. Soon the husks became chaff, and the rice lay bright and brown in a bamboo basket.

The strange rhythm of those heavy poles against the hollow trough lingered in our minds as we walked through the deep-blue dusk to the village elder's home for the meeting of the church. Runners had been sent to tell the members about the service.

The red-clay tile roof of the little house was held up with a network of bamboo poles. The walls were made of bamboo leaf and rice straw woven into mats. The room itself served the farmer as barn for his rice, garage for his Honda, dining room for his meals, and living room for his guests. Now it served as a meetinghouse for one of the thousands of little churches that have recently come alive in Indonesia.

The service opened with a ceremonial meal of rice cake and tea with about twelve men sitting around the table in the center of the room. The women and children and younger men sat in a circle on boxes and bags of rice. A few sat on the hard-packed earthen floor.

The deacon called for a hymn. The song was one of Java's own, written to fit the Javanese dialect and thought patterns. One of the older men read the Scriptures, and then they prayed again. The members spoke briefly about their Christian experiences, and the missionary was asked to preach. The service ended and the people left for their tiny homes, guided by tiny street lamps made of small jars with wicks drawn through cork. They were suspended on poles in front of the homes. One ingenious man had used old electric light bulbs with the brass end removed. I looked out the rear window of our Volkswagen bus as we drove away and watched these tiny lights disappear into the darkness.

Late into the night I thought about what I had seen—a church without a building or even a pastor in the traditional sense. Yet here was a church where fellowship, worship, mutual burden-bearing, and simple evangelism were the most prominent features. So frail and so insignificant, yet there it was, the body of Christ, unmistakable in its zeal and its interest. One of Paul's sayings came to mind, "To the intent that now unto the principalities and powers in heavenly places might be known by the church the manifold wisdom of God" (Eph. 3:10).

Is this the church Paul was talking about? Is this ragged congregation part of the intent of God? Are these simple farmers responsible for making known the manifold wisdom of God in heavenly places? From the Spirit the simple answer came: Yes. But how could so unsophisticated a group be the key to the coming of the kingdom of God? How could the rakings and scrapings of God's creation be responsible for so lofty a task?

Then from the Spirit another answer came, this time also in Paul's words, "For consider your call, brethren; not many of you were wise according to worldly standards, not many were powerful, not many were of noble birth; but God chose what is foolish in the world to shame the wise, God chose what is weak in the world to shame the strong, God chose what is low and despised in the world, even things that are not, to bring to nothing things that are, so that no human being might boast in the presence of God" (1 Cor. 1:26–29, RSV).

God's work is a people's movement. When it is conducted as such, it succeeds; and when it is not, it fails. It is as simple as that; God's kingdom belongs to the people, not to priests and prelates, not to councils and conventions, not to unions and boards. If the churches are strong, the kingdom is growing; if they are weak, it is failing. God has chosen the churches as the growing edge.

Have you ever watched a welder's torch cutting steel on a dark night? First you see a great orb of light and then the white blaze of the welding tip. Looking closer you see at the edge of the white blaze an intensely hot blue blaze. The blue blaze supports the white blaze, but the white blaze does the cutting. In the world of sin the churches do the cutting. They burn with the white heat of men and women moved by the Spirit of God. They are the flaming edges of God's presence on earth.

Roland Allen in commenting on the growth of the churches in the New Testament times said: "Paul did not seek particularly to attract the scholars, the officials, and the philosophers. He certainly did not address himself to them. If he did so once at Athens, he deliberately refused to take the course at Corinth. He himself says he did not receive many converts from those classes." [1] Allen quoted Bishop Lightfoot as saying, "From the middle and lower classes of society it seems possible that the church drew her largest reinforcements."

Surely it was not that Paul had no love or appreciation for the upper classes. From references in his letter to the wealthy Philemon and his generous words about "few Greek women of high standing" (Acts 17:12, RSV) at Berea and the "few of the leading women" (Acts 17:4, RSV) at Thessalonica we know better than that. It was rather that Paul found the common people ready to receive the gospel and to form themselves into churches. He did the very human and probably the very divine thing of striking where the iron was hot, and to use the figure Jesus used, of working where "the fields are already white for harvest" (John 4:35, RSV).

It remains this way until this very day. Churches willing to go to the masses, and to preach to the masses without condescension and patronization find ready responses. A recent study shows that in Latin America the Pentecostals who have worked almost exclusively among the masses have grown to an incredible number of about 3,104,535 since they first entered the fields. This compares to 1,252,434 for the old line denominations. The point here is that it takes a people's church to reach people, and a people's church is one made up of the same people is trying to win. One church cannot win all. It takes many churches of many different kinds. We must establish churches to meet the needs of those we are attempting to reach. It is essential that we send missionaries to Africa, yet finally it is the Africans that must win Africa. The same can be said of any group anywhere.

But what has all this got to do with "Share the Word Now"? Well, the Bible is the sharp two-edged sword that penetrates the heart and marks the basic life issues. It is the key that unlocks the human will. Denominations that would evangelize must see to it that the Bible is used as the medium of understanding between Christian and non-Christian groups. They must realize that until vast numbers of church members become enthusiastic for Bible study, there can be no decisive penetration for Christ. They must also realize that the church dividing and scattering is the way new churches are formed. Against this world's darkness, it is not one edge but many edges that are needed. The church in action is the church that is establishing other churches for the winning of people to Christ.

The Church Being

Frank Stagg said in reference to Paul's use of the word "body" to describe the church, "The analogy may be taken too literally but it cannot be taken too seriously." After all, it is only a figure; yet as a figure it has no substitute in telling us what the church is to Christ, or in portraying his dependence upon it. Stagg also makes clear that the body is not Christ, as some have believed, but that it is dependent on Christ as the head of the body. The body responds to the head, as wholly dependent upon it, and the head responds to the body as thought it had no other way for its work to be done. The body is dependent on the head for its fulness: "The Head, from whom the whole body, nourished and knit together through its joints and ligaments, grows with a growth that is from God" (Col. 2:19, RSV).

The other side of this is what Stagg calls Paul's daring thought, that Christ has been made "the head over all things for the church, which is his body, *the fulness of him* who fills all in all" (Eph. 1:22–23, RSV). Compare this with the words of Jesus in his long prayer to the Father, speaking of those who believed in him, he said, "All mine are thine, and thine are mine, *and I am glorified in them*" (John 17:10, RSV). Christ finds fulness and glory in the church. It is indeed a daring thought.

No wonder Paul saw the church as making known the wisdom of God to principalities and powers and as a depository of God's glory. As the body of Christ, it must take itself seriously, as the world also must take it seriously. Both Christ and the world are dependent upon it. The church must self-consciously, but not proudly, go about its business. It must plant itself again and again in strategic places as proclaimer and minister to the world. It proclaims the death and resurrection of Christ, and it ministers as a healer to all mankind.

"The Church Grows with a Growth That Is from God"

These simple words of Paul point to a truth sometimes hard for us to see, that the appearance and health of the church in the world is directly the responsibility of God. We are wrong to work at it or worry about it, as if it all depended on us. This is our temptation, and it is the reason we work too feverishly or don't work at all. We sometimes go about our church work as if we alone were responsible. This would be all right if we were not so self-righteous about it, and if we could leave more of the impression that we have a silent partner to carry the load and work the miracle. At other times we sit down and don't do anything because we are afraid we will fail and we don't want to be embarrassed.

This, of course, means that we have forgotten Christ as the secret of our power. After all it is not we who work, but Christ who works through us. For example, we don't visit for the church because we have too often gone in our own strength and not his, dependent on ourselves and not him and have failed. We don't want to fail again. We don't always believe Jesus who said, "My Father is working still, and I am working" (John 5:17, RSV). We had much rather pretend that it is all up to us and fail as to admit it is all up to God and succeed.

How can any human being, even the most devout church member ever assume that he can manipulate the growth of God's church? He can surrender to it, and become adjunct to it. He can help it along with his humility and his faith but he cannot will it or invent it, anymore than he can will the coming of spring or invent a seed. The more he tries to manipulate the more cynical and ridiculous he becomes.

This world has seen some preachers, misguided and unprincipled, who have been false prophets. These are the Simon the Sorcerers who would buy the Holy Spirit for a price (Acts 8:18 ff.). Simon had his gall of bitterness and his bond of iniquity. The miracle of it is that at the end such may be truly converted as was Simon the Sorcerer. This is because at the heart of the church lies the power of God to make all things new. The church itself is not the power, but Christ in the church, and he still is at work.

The idea of all church growth is spontaneity. This is the law of life, and the law of the spirit—spontaneity. Churches that really grow are responding spontaneously to the life of God in their midst. It is a spontaneity fed and nourished by a constant study of God's Word. This means that the church curiously alive to the Bible and searching it daily for the truth it offers is providing itself fuel for spontaneity. This is the yolk out of which the germ of life draws its nourishment. Bible study and prayer are the foods for growth. Effective work for Christ is possible only when there is spontaneity of the Spirit, nourished in the milk and meat of the Word.

"Night Cometh When No Man Can Work"

What I have said must not be taken as inferring that the church is not to work. My point has been that assumption on which the church does its work must be that Christ is both the power and the secret of success. Just because he works does not mean Christians are to quit working. When he healed the man born blind, he said, "We must work the works of him who sent me, while it is day; night comes, when no man can work" (John 9:4, RSV).

We are not merely doing our work for God in the world; rather, we are doing God's work, and he is working through us. Indeed he works *ahead of us* to prepare the way, *beside us* to help us, and *behind us* to correct the mistakes we make. The church has much work to do, and of course at the end the work of the church is the work of its individual members. On this point Paul speaks, "When each part is working properly, makes bodily growth and upbuilds itself in love" (Eph. 4:16, RSV).

"Each Part Working Properly"

The body of Christ is made up of parts "joined and knit together, together by every joint" (see Col. 2:19). One hesitates to compare a church with a circus, but it may not be so irreverent after all, especially if it is remembered that it is merely an illustration. Both are celebrating; the circus celebrates the physical achievements of man and the church celebrates the life of God in the midst. Both are rejoicing, the circus with a brass band and laughter and the church in psalms and with songs and prayers. Both are responding to something outside themselves, the circus to the idea of the circus, and the church to its living Head.

Both the circus and the church are moved by a spirit, the circus by the spirit that says the show must go on, the church by the Spirit of the Eternal God in its breast. Both are mobile, the circus performing either in a tent or in a room not its own, here today gone tomorrow, the church responding to the migrations of people and always recognizing that when its mobility is low, it is failing in its mission.

Both the circus and the church are people; with the circus the people are the performers; no performers, no circus. It is the same with the church; no people, no church; the body of Christ is dependent on people. With the circus, the people are skilled performers, already arrived at the peak of their profession. With the church, the people are a rag-tag group, in the process of being made perfect. With the circus, the cooperation of the people is essential to its success. When a man jumps from a swing, there must be another man to catch him. With the church also, the knitting together is essential. The circus dwindles and dies, but the church is eternal for "unto [God] be glory in the church by Christ Jesus throughout all ages, world without end" (Eph. 3:21).

The body of Christ is composed of many members, feet, hands, eyes, ears, or to put it another way, preachers, apostles, teachers, evangelists, ministers. And to put it still a different way, those who are wise, those who know, those who heal, and those who are renowned for their faith. The important thing is that they all work together, everyone in his place, from the star on the highest trampeze to the clown in the gaudiest garment, and if one falls the other is there to catch him. God has willed "that there be no discord in the body, but that the members may have the same care for one another. If one member suffers, all suffer together; if one member is honored, all rejoice together" (1 Cor. 12:25–26, RSV).

The church working may not always be the church at labor. Perhaps a better word than working is yeasting, for it is the yeasting of the church that will make most difference in the world. Yeasting is a relatively silent and unseen kind of working. It again is the spontaneity of God in our midst, and the thing which we most desperately need at the present.

Yeasting is the outgrowth of faith, not something we can automatically generate in the sense that we create the spore and the meal, and that we are responsible for the life. It comes from believing that God wants to work in the world and will work in the world if certain things are brought into proper relationship to each other. In yeasting for bread the woman's labor is to get the spore and the meal together. In yeasting for God, the labor of the church is to bring the fire and the truth of God's Word and the innumerable lost souls that are all about the world into relationship to each other. Somehow we must learn to labor where the Word has done its work and the yeasting is taking place, where the dough is growing, and the people are ready to respond spontaneously to God.

Ultimately the responsibility for work in the church belongs to the individual. God does not speak to us from a platform to the whole church, but through the still small voice to persons. He calls them by name and gives them an assignment. He says, "Look you there so smug and indifferent to the needs of the church, there is one of my jobs I want you to do." It may be people to visit or a class to be taught. It may be sick to be helped or strangers to be encouraged. To fail to respond to God's personal word to you, is to die a little and to fail the church. To respond is to grow a little and to add glory to the church. To respond is to run spontaneously with the feet of a deer through the rocky hills of life, to fail to respond is to wear leaden shoes in a sand bed.

The Church Growing

A church must grow two ways, one in the knowledge and spirit of Christ and the other in the number of members. These two things go together. To grow in the knowledge and spirit of Christ is to attract others into the fellowship, as the magnetism of iron attracts iron particles. Some churches appear to grow without any genuine knowledge of Christ. They flourish and appear to be successful, but their growth is based on a spurious foundation. It lacks the authenticity of Christian experience. Genuine Christian fellowship, in which Christ is encountered as a personal living presence, is the authentic edge of the church, the burning edge that grows.

The Place of Fellowship in Church Growth

In a small East Tennessee rural church, an aged pastor concluded his sermon with an invitation to the church to join him in a moment of fellowship. Nearly the whole congregation walked forward to stand around the pulpit. He then asked if anyone had anything to say to the church. One man thanked the church for its prayers for his wife. Another confessed a great burden and asked for prayers. One by one the people talked, even some of the youth. A woman lifted her praise to God and ended with a small shout. Only the visitors and the nonmembers did not join in the fellowship.

Standing there as a spectator, I felt I was looking at what a church ought to be, people close together, mutually supporting each other in a loving and caring fellowship. In a flash I also saw what it means for a church to be alive in its evangelistic appeal. Sitting alone on one pew far to the back was a young couple obviously under deep spiritual conviction. On another pew sat a middle-aged husband whose wife was standing with the church. He, too, was deeply moved in conviction.

All about were well-worn Bibles. Earlier in the Sunday School I had heard the low mumblings of a half-dozen classes in which the Scriptures were discussed. The pastor had preached a moving biblical sermon. Christ was present both in Word and in Spirit. Here, I thought, is the true growing edge of the church, "the edge of the edge" that pushes out into the darkness. As I watched and prayed, I thought of a similar experience in a Madrid church, where a hundred devoted Spanish Christians crowded the walls of a tiny back-alley building in a deep and happy fellowship. Now as I think of those two churches, I wonder if this is what Pentecost was like.

Contrast them with what took place in a recent Sunday night service where fifty people tried to worship in one of those pride-built auditoriums that seats five hundred, and that takes more than half of the church's income to meet the bank mortgage. Six people sat in the middle sections of pews, three children at the front row of the choir. The rest were sitting like sleepy owls in two little knots on the outside edges of the two side sections of pews. The pastor was nearly cross-eyed, trying to give his attention to that divided congregation.

When the strained sermon was ended and the group dismissed, the room emptied in less than one minute. Is it any wonder that two visitors present took their membership elsewhere?

The problem in this church is more than lack of Bible study, for there seems to be some of that. It is lack of spirit, specifically lack of the Spirit of Christ, partly because of a prideful and unrealistic building. Also, members have failed to see that Christian fire develops from a communicating fellowship in which the people develop a closeness to each other because Christ is present. It would be far better for that church to forget its Sunday night choir and its new organ, and meet in a small room where the fellowship could be given a chance to develop and deepen. Soon it would begin to attract people, and the crowd could move back into the sanctuary. It cannot do it with a dead, rigid and insensitive leadership.

The Place of Leadership in Church Growth

Churches do not grow without leaders. A recent study by six Latin American missionaries to determine what makes churches grow concluded that the first requirement is "dynamic, spirit-filled leaders." After investigating hundreds of churches and interviewing more than a thousand people, the missionaries noted that the successful church leader may be either a pastor or a layman. "God chooses to inspire his people through leaders," they said. A successful pastor's academic preparation may vary, "he shows that God has given him the gift of the ministry." The missionaries also found that the pastor gives strong evidence of divine call to his task. He plans and inspires his church with his plans. He visits and he inspires his people to march with him.

Much of the ministry of Jesus was devoted to leadership training. Frequently he would draw his closest disciples aside for talk. The special things he taught in these intimate conversations may still be the proper curriculum for training Christian leaders. The Sermon on the Mount, for example, was delivered only to the disciples. These teachings were revolutionary then, and they are revolutionary today. What a difference it would make if church leaders started truly practicing and teaching that marvelous discourse.

Jesus lifted his disciples up to heaven but he kept their feet on the ground and their lives in touch with the common people. So much of what he taught was from objects. He wrote in the sand; he sat a child in the midst of them; he asked for a coin; he overturned the money tables in the Temple; he pointed to the walls of the Temple; he entered Jerusalem on the back of an ass—all in effort to get his disciples to see the directness and the simplicity which religious leaders should use in reaching people. He no doubt knew what many fail to see: that most minds have difficulty in understanding abstract ideas. These were important and he never hesitated to speak them, but every time he could he made his truth come alive with some kind of object lesson.

Another quality he emphasizes was enthusiasm. He selected his disciples for their energy and initiative. He probably was the first man to say, "I'd rather hold them back than to have to push them forward." Except for one or two lapses the men he chose were on the go from the start. Peter spearheaded the church after Pentecost. John carefully noted everything Jesus said and did and wrote the marvelous Gospel that bears his name. Nathanael found his brother and brought him to Jesus. The disciples were constantly reaching out after others to bring them to their newly discovered truth.

The leaders who came later were also strong and enthusiastic. John Mark stood up to the great Paul when he thought he was wrong. He also wrote the first Gospel. Luke chronicled his Gospel and the Acts of the Apostles. James became the respected leader of the church at Jerusalem and the author of one of the great letters of the New Testament. Stephen faced a mob and Philip went out as an itinerant evangelist.

Paul confronted the whole Gentile world and preached to kings. He once said in reference to the resurrection, "I press toward the mark for the prize of the high calling of God in Christ Jesus" (Phil. 3:14). This lofty language was consistent with Paul's loyalty and enthusiasm for his cause. He pressed on all his life to Pamphylia, to Galacia, to Macedonia, to Jerusalem, to Rome, to Spain. Paul and the other early leaders are examples in enthusiasm for all Christian leaders.

Two churches exist side by side. One has a fine building but no people. The other has scores of young families and hundreds of people, but a modest building. The difference in the two may be attributed to leadership. One pastor is dour and retreating. He has kind of an institutional view of the ministry that makes him appear to be serving the organization. His vision of his role does not derive from the New Testament but from how the ministry appeared to him as a child. He claims to major on preaching, but his sermons, supposedly well prepared are compilations of ideas he has drawn from commentaries. They do not burn because he does not burn. He lacks insight into people because he has never allowed himself to be with people and to draw from people. His church is dying for lack of leadership.

The other church grows because of leadership. Its pastor, through an older man than the other, seems to live the Bible in his contact with people. He studies hard, but is in no sense a recluse, for he mingles with his members at the level of experience. He is human but he carries the mark of belonging to Christ. His vision of the ministry derives from both the New Testament and his understanding of the needs of the people. He is successful because he derives his message from the Scriptures, he keeps it down to earth, and he is enthusiastic for his cause. Is it any wonder that his church grows?

The Church Extending

At Christmas we hang glass ornaments and flashing lights on evergreen trees. These baubles are not the fruit of the trees. As Christians we are always in danger of decorating the church with things which are not the fruit of faith. They may satisfy our pride but they do not add to the kingdom of God. The evergreen tree of the church bears many kinds of genuine fruits, among them the mutual burden-bearing of its members, the loyalty of its people to its purpose, and such graces as love, kindliness, peace and joy.

Two other fruits are extremely important—new Christians added to its fellowship, and new congregations in other locations. God has willed that the church must always be dispersing into new areas, contacting new people, transplanting itself in new environments. If it becomes rigid and inflexible and holds stubbornly to the forms and places of the past, it soon dies, a vine without fruit, destroyed with its own barrenness.

In one of his sermons, Daniel T. Niles quoted John R. Mott as saying that the main problem in the church's life was that its forces were immobile. Niles comments: "The church in its encounter with the world and its service to the world and its witness in the world, had in many places planted heavy institutions and had adopted intricate procedures of work. To put it in another way, the church was prepared for trench warfare but found itself faced with an enemy whose methods were much more flexible. There is no use in meeting challenges which are not there, and in being silent at those places where the actual questions are being asked, where the actual problems have to be met." [2]

Some of the satellites sent into space have self-destruction devices. After they have served their usefulness, they disintegrate. It is said that cars are built with obsolescent features. After terms of dependable service, they begin a kind of engineered deterioration. Perhaps some local churches also should have such features. After a long and glorious service they should divide and disperse, as the church in Jerusalem did, into other communities where opportunities are greater.

As a matter of fact, this does happen in some instances: churches flourish, expand, reach high-water marks, then as their communities change, they die, unless of course they change with the communities. Some do not know they are dead, and linger on to give the cause a black eye, most of the time tied to a building which was built by a proud congregation for a future that never materialized. The remnant is a kind of living corpse in an elegant and backward-looking mausoleum. It has forgotten that the true church always sees itself as a tabernacle, not a temple, as a tent, not a palace.

This is not to be taken as a criticism of permanent and beautiful buildings. Emphatically they are most desirable and essential. Nor is it to denigrate the older churches. Great buildings and old churches bring strength and dignity to the kingdom of God, especially when they adapt to the times. We must presume all of them. The point I am stressing is the need for highest mobility. A church should never be so tied to a place or a building that it cannot reestablish itself in the midst of the people wherever they are. Sometimes it can do this from its present premises, sometimes it cannot. The denomination that is without an active church extension program is gradually dying.

Why New Congregations Are Necessary

The churches must win souls to Christ, and the vehicle for this is

86

the teaching of the Bible. Unless the Bible is taught to the multitudes, they are not likely to be won. For thirty years Billy Graham has had phenomenal success in evangelism. God has given him rare ability and wisdom. But Graham also has had going for him the faithful teaching of the Bible in thousands of churches for two hundred years. Think how much harder his job would have been without the churches. America has been a people whose consciousness has been largely molded by the Bible. But is this as true as it once was? Some people think not.

In fact the rapid increase in population, the failure of Sunday Schools to grow, and the creeping influence of secularism has created a kind of unsympathetic national community. Our only hope is to take the actions that will bring the Bible back to the people. One of these is for the churches to reestablish themselves in a multitude of missions in reach of every human being.

The mobility of the people demands a respondent mobility of the churches. The constant relocation of families is one of the social facts of modern times. In the five years from 1965 to 1970, 47 percent of all Americans changed residences. This has been going on for the past quarter of a century. Not everyone moves, of course, and some move often. The transitory nature of our nation means new communities are constantly being formed.

The only way churches can meet this phenomena is to divide and conquer. They must recognize their own itinerant character and move to reestablish themselves in new congregations wherever the people live.

We have considered two reasons why new congregations are needed. One is in order to put a Bible-teaching center in the midst of the people and two, because the people themselves are mobile and need a respondent mobile church. Make maximum use of old buildings, but build new ones too.

A third reason is more complex but just as important. For fifty years there has been a running argument on the subject of class churches. Is it right to have a mill church made up of nothing but mill workers? What about churches for bankers, for merchants, for country club classes, for middle classes? Most people have assumed such churches did not truly represent the kingdom of God and that all churches ought to have members from all classes.

Perhaps ideally this is true, but does it square with the actual social milieu in which we must live? We know all churches ought to be open to all people and classes; yet we also know that most classes do not readily and quickly mix. Donald A. McGavaran in his monumental *Bridges of God* says, "To ignore the significance of race hinders Christianization. It makes an *enemy* of race consciousness, instead of an ally." McGavaran is not pleading for segregation, for his whole life's ministry has been against that. Nor is he taking a narrow, provincial view of the church. He is arguing for a special kind of growth strategy. He strongly believes that the group, whether racial or ethnic or class group, is a dominant force in the rapid growth of churches, and that individuals respond to group leadership. He argues that we should be extremely aware of the social integrity of any group we are trying to win, and make the group our ally.

McGavaran's thesis is based on the thought of Roland Allen, a missionary to China, who believed that early Christian leaders moved in response to groups as well as to individuals. One example is Paul's use of synagogues and his work in cities that had strong Jewish communities. He was sensibly striking where religious understanding was highest and the iron the hottest. The point is this: Americans have high physical mobility, and they also have an extremely high social mobility. They are always forming into new groups and new communities.

We should be extremely realistic in recognizing the impossibility of maintaining churches without strong group or community bases. We should move to establish churches where there is room to grow within a group, and where the group becomes ally, not enemy. Some denominations are moving to establish apartment house churches in response to this new strategy.

The Way New Congregations Are Started

Most churches that have effectively met the need for new congregations have centered their expansion in the Bible, either through the establishment of home Bible fellowships which led to full-grown Sunday Schools in which the Bible was taught to all ages, or through the establishment of Sunday Schools as a first step. The need for the teaching of the Bible determines the strategy.

While we would not want to push the point very far, there is a sense in which to be the church is to teach. The church cannot survive unless it is repeating over and over again what it is all about. It must teach in its own premises, to its own kind, and to others, but if it teaches others, it must become a church not merely *for* others, but *of* others. If it cannot teach the multitudes in its present premises, then it must find other premises where it can teach. Finding these new premises for teaching, homes, stores, barber shops, chicken houses, schools, bars, offices, hotels, wherever people gather, this is the inevitable business of the church. It is the task for a special breed of Christians, men and women whom God has called to pioneer in his work. Not all can do it, but the ones who can do it, certainly should.

A missionary in Africa, living in a remote inland city, one day rode his Jeep as far as there was any road. He then walked through the forests and came to a valley. High on the next hill he saw the smoke of a village. He pressed on to the village, and there in the last house he taught the Scriptures and formed a church. He then said that he realized that out beyond, over the hill was another village, so walking again for miles, he came once more to the last house in the last village and formed yet another church. This willingness to press on to the outer limits, to go to the uttermosts, is what it takes for churches to keep on reestablishing themselves in all of the world. The motivation is Jesus Christ, the method is a Bible in hand that must be shared.

Some denominations have numerous men who have spent their lives organizing new churches. They would not do anything else, because they have found satisfactions in seeing churches come alive and grow. They are not in the glass bauble business, and they do not find their fulfilment in hanging false fruit on the tree of the church. They live in a world of Christian reality and daily die to secure the kingdom of God in new communities.

What they build may appear to be nothing more than a loose confederation of believers in an Indonesian bamboo church, but it is the body and bride of Christ, the growing edge of God's kingdom, the sweet perfume of Christ's presence, the temple of God in a strange land, and from it an irresistible appeal will go forth, until the gospel covers the whole earth as the waters cover the sea.

When Von Worten drives his Volkswagen bus into the Indonesian countryside, he is going in search of souls. He is armed with the

Scriptures as God's treasury of truth. He shares it with any who will stop and listen. As they listen, he notes when they are open and ready to accept Christ. When enough have heard and believed, a church is formed and left in the care of the Holy Spirit. This is no game of "cross questions and crooked answers." It is truth marching. With the Bible and the Holy Spirit the church is kept alive and working. What emerges in these new congregations is the body and the bride of Christ, the new holy temple, the resident of God's truth on earth. Like Von Worten, you and I must keep pressing the battle to the gates, not doing Christ's work for him, but standing alongside Christ and becoming his partner as he does his work through us. We can always do it better with the Bible in hand and heart.

6] [The Word in Dialogue with the World

One of the exciting books to appear lately is *The Big Little School* by Robert W. Lynn and Elliot Wright. The authors say, "Denominations have established hundreds of colleges and universities, but the Sunday School is the *big* school in religious matters for the Protestant people. . . . Compared to public education Sunday School is marginal to American society, yet is an important little school in the rearing of the whole nation. The Sunday School is the big little school of the United States." [1]

Where did the big little school start?

Some students think it was in Savannah, Georgia, in 1735 when young John Wesley gathered children together on Sunday to teach the Scriptures. Most believe that the beginning was in England in the 1780's when Robert Raikes began to promote "ragged schools" for the poor children of the industrial cities. He had heard farmers and merchants complain of more vandalism on Sunday than all the other days of the week put together. He reasoned that the hordes of youth who worked in factories could be taught to read the Scriptures on Sunday, relieving the people of their vandalism, lifting up the children's preparation for life, and preparing them to be Christians. His movement caught fire and spread all over England.

In 1785 William Fox, a pious leader, Baptist, and a businessman, along with several other influential men helped launch the first organization for promoting Sunday Schools. He raised money to hire teachers, provide Bibles and appoint school visitors. By 1787 enrolment in England stood at 250,000 children.

The movement also caught fire in America.

It spread everywhere, even into the pioneer west. By around 1830 a young fur trader in St. Louis wrote his mother in Connecticut: "An excitement has gone forth. An excitement that the power of man can neither gainsay or put down. It exists not in the East alone. It has past the boundary which separates the East from the Western states. It has reached this place."

At times it was vigorously opposed. George Daughaday, a Methodist minister in Charleston, South Carolina, was drenched with water from the public cistern when he attempted to organize a Sunday School for black boys and girls. But it was too late to stop the rolling tide that soon covered the nation with Sunday Bible schools for whites and blacks alike, as well as for Indians and other minority groups.

In the 150 years since the first excitement of the big little schools in America, the movement has continued to grow until today there are 139,662 Sunday Schools, enrolling 42,000,000 people and occupying 798 million square feet of floor space.

Sunday Schools still have their detractors and maligners. At the beginning of the twentieth century critics forecast its demise, and even sophisticated leaders felt it had outlived its usefulness. Lynn and Wright say: "A few conscientious observers at the world Sunday School Parade in 1910 (Washington, D.C.) would happily have sung, 'Shall We Gather at the River' one last time and laid the 'Army of the Lord' to rest in the Arlington National Cemetery."

But the Sunday School movement did not die. It still lives, hail and hearty, and as determined as ever. Particularly among conservative groups, it is alive. Some of the possible reasons for this are (1) it is promoted as the evangelistic arm of the church, (2) the quality and intensity of leadership training has steadily improved, (3) the conservative Sunday Schools put considerable emphasis on Bible classes for adults, (4) the construction of tens of thousands of classrooms gives the Sunday School adequate and modern meeting places of their own, (5) the broadening of the Sunday School to include social and fellowship needs of its members, and (6) the traditional Sunday School is now a Bible school with newly developed Bible study fellowships.

What is the future of the Sunday School?

There are still a few detractors, and the Sunday School carries a dead weight in the indifference of some of its leaders. Most leaders heartily believe that it will be around a long long time, aided by innovative supporting programs like Vacation Bible School and Weekday Bible classes.

The real hope may lie in dynamic Bible study that spills over from the church on Sunday into organized Bible study fellowships in the homes of the people during the week. These informal groups called "Bible study fellowships" show signs of becoming (1) the most suitable evangelistic door for the present, (2) a way of meeting the inconvenience of the shift hours of modern labor practice, (3) the best way to start new Sunday Schools in new locations, (4) a successful way to achieve in-depth Bible study, and (5) a way to show persons timid about coming to church what Christian fellowship is all about.

Bible Study Fellowships As Koinonia Groups

Successful Bible study fellowships must be more than meetings of people to discuss the Scriptures. If they are to contribute to the living stream of evangelism, they must take on that essential fire of the church often called *koinonia* in the Greek New Testament and best translated with the word "fellowship." Sometimes *koinonia* is used to describe the intimate relationship believers and God have which is mediated through Jesus Christ; other times it is used to describe the sweet companionship of Christians at work in worship and ministry; and other times to describe the loving concern of the strong for the weak. *Koinonia* is not a gathering of congenial people, but the gathering of a special people in whom the Spirit of Christ is at work. P. S. Minear said, "They are the joint heirs of a common life bestowed by him (Christ) through the Spirit." In this special kind of Christian fellowship, loyalty to the group does not derive from duty but from love.

Bible study fellowships must become true *koinonia* groups for them to survive and become effective. Their purpose is not merely to study the Bible but to study the Bible in order to build the community of faith. The presence of the Scriptures in the group helps open the way to fellowship. It is not quite like a group studying Tolstoy's *War and Peace,* for with them Tolstoy is not present. With people who prayerfully study the Bible together, Christ is always present.

Howard Grimes in his book *The Rebirth of the Laity* says that three principles are essential for the formation of true fellowship groups. The group (1) must be small enough for personal interaction, (2) sufficiently disciplined for order to be maintained, (3) structured so as to accomplish its purpose. These can all be applied to Bible study fellowships.

Small Enough for Personal Interaction

How big should a Bible fellowship be in order to secure good interaction between its members? When does it become too big? It is not a case of thinking small or thinking big but of keeping the groups the right size for personal interchange and fellowship. Groups can be composed of two people, as we see in the experience of Philip and the eunuch. When Philip saw this black man in his chariot, he stepped up beside him and asked him if he understood what he was reading. An interchange took place and a group was formed, knit together by the Holy Spirit.

Philip's skill is handling the interview reminds us that the really critical thing is not the size of the group, but what takes place. Skill in leadership is much more important than the numbers of the fellowship. Some leaders work better with large numbers, and some with smaller numbers.

Another factor in the size of the group is the kind of agenda the group is following. The more involved in the agenda, the smaller the group because fewer people can participate in a complicated procedure. As agendas change, the size of the groups may also change. A skilful leader in Bible study will find ways of involving more people as his class becomes larger.

The diversity of a Bible study fellowship may also control its size, especially at first. The more diverse people are, the more successful the enterprise will be, if it is kept small. Of course, as its members are assimilated, its numbers can increase. C. Burtt Potter, Jr., established thirteen groups in Philadelphia, most of which had a diverse membership: "Informal fellowships attract all kinds . . . enthusiasts inclined toward speaking in tongues, unbelievers, Bible scholars and Bible illiterates, emotionally starved and those whom we call normal."

If this seems like a strange group to be brought together in Christian fellowship, then compare it with the diverse group of disciples Jesus brought together. Note also that Jesus molded these twelve men into a group fellowship before adding the 120. It is important that as a group increases in size that the group spirit grows with it.

One authority on Christian group dynamics says, "Twelve may be a maximally productive group, though a group may be smaller and,

I believe as large as twenty or slightly more. Indeed certain qualities of good group life may come into being when there are twenty-five or thirty; and it is our hope that to some extent an entire congregation may realize its potential as a community. Six to eighteen is probably the range of maximum productivity, however, and some would insist on a maximum of seven or eight." [2]

The real criteria for group size is the quality of interchange. A Sunday School class, for example, that never opens for discussion is too big even though you have one monologuing teacher and five members. On the other hand it is possible for a hundred or more people to live in dynamic interchange provided as you have the right leader. Only as interchange starts moving can the Spirit of God take over to form *koinonia*.

Sufficiently Disciplined for Order to Be Maintained

Discipline as it is used here does not refer to the department of its members as in a school, or the enforced regimentation of members as in the army. Bible study fellowships could not survive long under such restrictions. It does refer to an orderly process, the most single important feature of which is purpose.

A disciplined group knows where it is going. It does not waste time in tediously debating the reasons for its existence. When it convenes, it knows what to do. On this point Howard Grimes says, "It cannot wander at will, whether it be a planning group or a study group." A group that forms and then tries to find out why it is in business is not truly a group and never will be. Imagine, if you will, a group of alcoholics trying to find out why they are together. Their search will lead them back to the bottle. On the other hand, imagine a group of desperate alcoholics who have come longingly to Alcoholics Anonymous. They know immediately what to do, and in doing it they find solidarity and sobriety.

A Bible study fellowship knows where it is going. The means, the methods, the possibilities of a Bible study fellowship may not be the same for one group as they are for another but the purposes are always the same. There are three of them: (1) To study the Bible in such a way as to find solidarity in Christ. (2) To form other Bible study fellowships. The successful fellowship will divide and create more fellowships. (3) To become a church or at least part of a church.

The Bible study fellowship, disciplined by purposes, does not exist by and for itself. John L. Casteel says: "Its true life is to be found in the church. Although at the beginning, a group may have little connection with the church, and although it may find that keeping itself centered in the life of the church is beset by many problems, still the church is its goal, heaven and home, and it moves toward the larger frame of worship and service as steadily as it can." [3]

A disciplined group is made up of committed members. "Personal groups do not depend upon exceptional abilities or strong personalities either to get started, or to continue and grow. They depend upon committed men and women." If the Bible study fellowship movement really catches on, it will be due to the Holy Spirit moving in the hearts of the believers. The tiny group meeting in homes, in schools, in hotels, in businesses, and in scores of other places derive both their strength and their discipline from the deep sense of "oughtness" that seize the members. Like Paul, they are "apprehended of Christ" (Phil. 3:12). The same Spirit that brings them together provides the glue to keep them together.

Structured as to Accomplish Their Purpose

It is true that Bible study fellowships depend on committed men and women for their discipline, but this does not mean they are without form or leadership, both of which are essential for the orderly realization. The form is simple and the leadership is informal.

Leadership is also essential, though it should not be obstructive or presumptuous. A Bible study fellowship is not an opportunity for a Bible student to lecture on the Scriptures. There is no room for dramatics or oratory in this program. The leader as a rule should be chose by his church, but nevertheless himself have a commitment to his task. He should find strange new people stimulating and enjoy know them for their own sakes. He should be schooled in the Scriptures, and skilled in the conversational method of teaching.

Bill Glass, formerly a professional football player and now an evangelist, has described a Bible study fellowship in a way that points up its *koinonia* and learning possibilities most graphically: "When I joined the Cleveland Browns in 1962, I shared with others the wonderful privilege of showing three different players on the team what it meant to be a Christian. Jim Ray Smith, a teammate of theirs, had lived the Christian life before them and they had become vitally interested. It was important that these three young Christians have a proper foundation in the Christian life.

"We started with a Bible study fellowship group and met every Friday night in a different home. There were six couples that met together—the Shofners, the Smiths, Mavis and I, and the three couples who had just become Christians; and we continued this fellowship group all through the playing season. After supper together we would begin our discussion group. We started with prayer. I was the group leader, but I tried not to talk any more than anyone else. Each member of the group discussed a passage of Scripture.

"For example, we worked through Ephesians, taking one chapter each night. We rewrote the chapter in our own words, averaging eight words per verse. If there were ten verses in a chapter, we had an eighty word total in our summary. When we rewrote the passage in our own words, we were surprised at how well we came to know the passage. The apostle Paul has some introductions to his letters. In our attempts to rewrite his introduction in the most contemporary English, we'd just say 'Hi!' We felt that this was what he was trying to get across in our modern day language." [4]

Bible Study Fellowships As the Growing Edge of the Church

Tomorrow's churches?

Some say they will be only a shell of the past, others that they will go underground and others that they will not be here at all. Predictions like these come not only from our enemies, but also from our friends.

But what does this prove?

Nothing when placed against the two thousand-year history of churches. We have had our ups and downs and have pulled through stronger than ever. Not always exactly in the same form, but bolder and more forceful in confrontation with the world. We fully expect this to happen again. Some of our old habits and traditions may disappear but not the churches themselves. They are here to stay. All true believers confidently accept the promise of Christ, "I will build my church; and the gates of hell shall not prevail against it" (Matt. 16:18).

None need be surprised that the churches change, for that is their

97

nature. Anything that moves changes, and the churches are always moving. Gilbert W. Stafford says that the churches "are called to be aware of; to be sensitive to and to participate in the divine movement of God." God moves, and the churches move with him. Stafford also says that the movement is

1. of God through Christ *to the world,*
2. of God through Christ *in the world,*
3. of people through Christ *to God,*
4. of people through Christ *to people,* and
5. of people *toward fulfilment.*

R. Eugene Sterner in commenting on this says, "Such a concept of the church is dynamic rather than static terms, as ministry rather than organization, as mission rather than institution, challenges many of our assumptions and sets us on the road to adventure."

The churches in adventurous movement means that they are always breaking outside themselves into the world. When a church finally goes to the world, a radical movement takes place. Hendrick Kraemer wrote, "Every Christian needs two conversions: first to Christ and then to the world." The continuing survival of the churches depends on their conversion to the world, their willingness to break outside themselves and to take their truth into the lives of those who resist it most.

Though it is too early to tell, it may be that Bible study fellowships are God's new way of pushing the churches out of their complacency into the highways and hedges. They may become the most practical way for the churches to fulfil the New Testament mandate to extend themselves into the world. Indeed, it appears that in their simplest form Bible study fellowships were the basic growth methods used in the first century of the church.

Dynamic Rather than Static

Robert A. Raines says, "The church must be the church in its own inner life before it can begin to be the church in the world." By this he seems to mean that before one can find others he must be found himself, before he can minister to others he must be ministered unto or before he can speak the Word to others, he must be spoken to by the Word. "Rarely does a person burst forth in personal ministry," Raines says, "who has not been awakened and nourished by the beloved fellowship."

The home base for a Bible study fellowship should always be a church, but the movement is always from the church to the world as leaders form groups in their homes, at work, at school, and in other places. The inspiration and strength for this bursting forth must always be from the church. Nevertheless there is a sense in which the church realizes its own inner life by breaking forth into the world. After all Philip's tiny Bible study fellowship in the chariot of the Ethiopian eunuch strengthened the church at Jerusalem, and Lydia's Bible study fellowship by a Macedonian river strengthened the churches in Asia.

It is a two-way street with blessings flowing both ways.

David Ernsberger in his book *Reviving the Local Church* tells of Alan Walker, pastor of the Central Methodist Mission in Sydney, Australia, who draws together each weekday noon many of the important decision makers of the city in what he calls the "Crossroads Club." "Walker's intention is to meet with them at the point of their special competence and concerns in the world, in their full secular integrity. The subjects under discussion in the group are the key issues emerging in the life of the city. The dialogue with the gospel to discover the concrete meaning of the lordship of Christ is thus initiated by events occurring in the metropolitan area where these men have responsibility." [5] Those study fellowships on the firing line of contemporary life represent the church dynamic, pulling it out of its walls into the marketplace of reality.

Ministry Rather than Organization

It is thoughtless for Christians to talk down the church as organization. Even a casual reading of the New Testament will reveal systematic structures in the early churches. They had pastors and deacons and did committee work and even counted their members. In the centuries since, the churches have been organized, often reflecting the kind of societies in which they lived and worked; for example, in a relatively unstructured frontier community the church was much less complicated than in a highly complex urban community. We must not let our detractors who talk as though church organization is evil, go unchallenged and uninstructed. After all Paul said, "Let all things be done decently and in order" (1 Cor. 14:40). There cannot be any doubt that this included structured churches.

All of this is one side of the question.

The other side is that the churches ought to work in such ways that the people see their essential spiritual character and not their organizations. Some critics say the church is too institutional, and they are right if the face it offers to the public is organization rather than ministry. There is a sense in which the church ceases to be the church, if only the organization is seen by the public. Always its manifestation to the world should be seen in its movement to the world in ministry and mission. It must be seen as doing something, not merely sitting there. Yet its work must be God's work, with him as the power and secret of the success.

Many sincere leaders believe the Bible study fellowship is the answer. These groups serve as tables that are set with bread and meat for the hungry, not temporal food, but spiritual food for a needy world. These tables serve the meat of which Jesus spoke: "Labour not for the meat which perisheth, but for that meat which endureth unto everlasting life, which the Son of man shall give unto you: for him hath God the Father sealed" (John 6:27). And of which Simon Peter spoke: "Silver and gold have I none; but such as I have give I thee: in the name of Jesus Christ of Nazareth rise up and walk" (Acts 3:6).

Bible Study Fellowship as Mission Rather than Institution

What is the church doing in the world, promoting itself or accomplishing mission?

The true answer to that question is "*Both* promoting itself *and* accomplishing mission." The promotion of itself is for the accomplishment of mission, for without the church as the visible body of Christ, people cannot see what it is that they are being asked to join. As visibility, the church is institutional and has form and shape. It can be described and pointed to, and at times advocated and even defended. Jesus surely was pointing to its institutional character when he said, "I build my church." But it is not institutional in the sense of banks and schools, but more in the sense of organized societies.

The church is sometimes underinstitutionalized, as when idealists talk of the church hidden in society, and they sometimes are overinstitutionalized as when they are thought of as synonymously with a building. The ideal church is neither a jellyfish without shape, nor concrete box without life; it is rather a living organism of committed believers in dialogue with the world. In fact unless in Christ's name there is humble dialogue with the world and fellowship with other Christians, the church is overinstitutionalized and in danger of suffocating in its own righteousness. Young people who are accusing the church of being overinstitutionalized are reacting against its lack of humble dialogue with the world.

Every church must fight to maintain dialogue. For a hundred years the strategy for dialogue has been to invite non-Christians into its premises for Bible study and evangelism. This has worked well, and still works for thousands of churches, and hundreds of thousands of people, but the time has come when in order to reach the masses another strategy is needed, one that keeps alive the movemental noninstitutional character of the church, one that shows it to be a fellowship of concern, willing to begin its work with the people wherever they are to be found. Many churches are discovering Bible study fellowships to be the answer to this needed new strategy.

A Bible study fellowship by communicating with non-Christians becomes the church in mission. It shows that the mission of God's love reaching out to the world is much greater than the church; yet it builds the church and in this way it accomplishes the mission. It is an evangelistic mission that edges boldly into the non-Christian community taking with it the fire and the life of the church.

Bible Study Fellowship as a Way for Church Spiritual Adventure

In Tampa, Florida, there is a housing center for retired people called Re-adventure. The promoters are appealing to the sense that most modern people have of wanting a new excitement. Psychologically, America is more inclined to engage in challenging new experiences than it has ever been. Impact of television, acceleration of change, and vast personal mobility lead most people to expect and to accept new ideas. The churches must take advantage of this trend by abandoning their customary reactionary roles and establishing bold new structures for augmenting their work.

Some of us remember World War II when all of America was mobilized to meet the enemy. Though it was a sad discouraging time, excitement was in the air, especially in the military training camps.

Hundreds of thousands of men remember the stimulating excitement of those days—new uniforms, new friends, new skills, new strengths, new purpose, and above all a sense of growth. Boys became men and resolutely faced the enemy. It was high adventure that nobody wanted; yet it was adventure and excitement as gradually the enemy was subdued.

As Christians we need this kind of challenge. We need to feel that we have a giant step to take, and that we must prepare to take it. Robert Raines pictures the congregation as the local headquarters for training the army of the Lord. He says: "It is the base of operations for the soldiers of Christ in that place. It is their drill hall, their strategy clinic, their hospital for the wounded and beaten, their center for regrouping and shaping new plans for defense and attack. Above all, it is the focal point where Christians are equipped for mission. Just as the logistics and organizational superstructure of an army are solely the means of preparing it for its varied missions, so the institutional paraphernalia of the local congregation are solely the means for preparing Christ's soldiers for their mission."

Some may think this analogy is a little too extreme, but they need not, especially if they keep in mind that it is only an analogy. The church is not a military base, but it is like a military base in that it equips Christians for service. It prepares the workers for exciting adventure in God's work of reconciling the world unto himself. Paul understood and used this analogy: "Put on the whole armor of God . . . the breastplate of righteousness . . . the shield of faith . . . the helmet of salvation . . . the sword of the Spirit" (Eph. 6:11–17, RSV). He spoke also of fighting the good fight. The church must always be the training base, but the battle must be fought in the world.

To talk of the death of the organized church that meets inside its own four walls for stated hours of worship and for training is to take an almost pathological stand on its future. At best such talk reveals a pessimistic spirit and a misunderstanding of the spiritual and social forces that give the church its present-day form. The spiritual forces derive from Christ's presence with us and his promise to build the church in such a way that the gates of hell shall not prevail against it.

The social forces derive from the way present-day life is organized. We have many public structures of nongovernmental nature which the people build and to which they pledge their loyalty. The church is free to be one of them. It stands in the community as a free institution because its members care enough to build it and support it. Throughout our long history, churches have been built by people who put them first in their lives. They supported the church, not because it was a convenient choice, but because it was preeminent in God's sight.

Those who predict the church's death seem to assume that it will cease to be preeminent and become an institution of convenience, and that it will take an inferior place among its members. The answer to this is the dedication of its members. As long as society is organized as it is now and the church is one of its options, then there will be people who will put it first.

This does not mean that the churches will not change, or that they will not sometimes be in trouble. It does mean that the church as a public institution will continue to exist despite the pathological predictions, and that as long as it exists it will be the training base for Christians in dialogue with the world. One way of being certain of an outpost ministry to the world is to establish Bible study fellowships, and let them be active organisms for action for Christ.

The Word of God Shared with the World

In training for service in the world, one important point to remember is that the Bible speaks to each generation from a new and different perspective. H. Richard Neibuhr wrote, "More light is always to break forth from the Scriptures; new occasions will teach new duties." The world moves, and so does God's response to it. This is why the churches must always be making new plans, writing new pamphlets, restating their ideas and replanning their strategies. The Holy Spirit keeps nudging the churches to do their work where the action is taking place, to make their witness at the crossroads of men. It is as if God is saying to the churches, "There where the world is burning, go set the Word of God in the midst of the fire." Bible study fellowships will always be where the fire is burning the brightest.

There are many ways the Word of God can be set to work where the world is burning. More churches are beginning to make the most of these ways, teaching them and setting up projects for implementation. Some of them are as follows:

1. *Mission action.* There are millions of people of special need and circumstances beyond the immediate reach of the church. They live in nursing homes, in prisons or in remote inaccessible communities. They work on Sundays in hospitals, dairies and factories. They are the socially estranged, such as the migrants, the minorities, and the poor. There is in all communities scores of places where these people are waiting for some friendly open friendship from the churches. One church conducts vocational classes in food preparation, ceramics, and decoupage in a women's prison. As the women work together, they talk about the gospel. Another church conducts Sunday morning worship services in the hotels of a resort area for benefit of vacationers, some of whom never go to church anywhere. Another church has organized Bible study fellowships in a nursing home.

2. *Personal ministry.* Every church needs an organized personal ministries program. It can do this through the various organizations, but especially through the Sunday Schools whose task it is to teach the Bible to all people of the community. Despite the fact that privacy is harder and harder to come by, a great loneliness is gripping the lives of most people. The sick and the infirm, the aged and the grieving many times suffer excruciating loneliness that others cannot seem to see or understand. Church members can be trained to help them. A covered-dish when death comes, a basket of flowers and a magazine for the sick room, an hour's visit to a nursing home, an afternoon of laundry work for helpless old people, letters to people in prison—the list can be as long as this book.

Wherever we go in personal ministry we should remember to take the Word of God with us, not in an obtrusive and vulgar manner, and often only as a Bible quotation. Alexander Whyte was very skilful in using the Bible in this way. Once after listening to a recital of the sufferings of a woman dying with an uncurable disease, he quoted Isaiah 40:31: "On eagles wings they mount, they soar." Then pausing at the door he said, "Put that under your tongue and suck it like a sweetie."

3. *Personal evangelism.* Perhaps the thing for which Christians are most responsible, they do the least—bearing their witness for Christ to non-Christians. Hopefully churches are beginning to train their members in personal soul-winning. Thousands of laymen are becoming active in presenting the gospel face to face to other people. One

man recently won another to Christ talking to him through the screen door, and another faithful worker won a young man while the youth's car continued to run.

The churches who continue to win people to Christ practice cultivation evangelism. One church assigns four or five couples to a man and wife team at the beginning of a new year, and faithfully trains the pair in how to make friends and how to draw the new couple into a group.

4. *Involvement in public life.* There is high adventure for Christians who see themselves as pilgrims for Christ at work in the various social and business structures of the community. One devout layman considers his job as mayor a fulfilment of his Christian commitment. A woman serves faithfully as a group lady in a local hospital in answer to the call of her church for community involvement. A minister serves on a local racial relations committee in call to his Christian conscience. These people are most faithful in sharing God's Word with those people with whom they are involved.

5. *Daily work.* Another battleline for dialogue with the world is the daily work environment. Most church members work among non-Christians and have endless opportunities to exemplify the life of Christ, and to speak a tactful word to someone about being a Christian. There are many noontime Bible study fellowships in offices and factories.

6. *Special projects.* One church operates a half-way house to help people find new lives after being in prison; and one operates a similar project to youth recovering from narcotic addiction. Another church maintains an off-premises coffeehouse for youth. Scores of churches maintain missions for people living in underprivileged areas, in which classes in homemaking and child care are offered along with Bible study.

Re-adventure

A knock on the door brought one of the most unruly young men of the church into the pastor's presence: "I don't know what I believe or how to tell it," he said. The pastor lent him a copy of the New Testament in a modern version. The summer went by but the boy never came to see the pastor. One day he finally appeared with the book swelled to twice its size and marked on every page. He also had a new copy of the same book which he gave to the pastor. "I want to keep this one, not just because I dropped it in the bathtub when I was reading it, but because it has changed my life." He then told how he had interested three other boys in Bible study and now the four had gotten permission from the high-school principal to organize Bible study fellowships for other youth at the noon hour. This, of course, is the repetition of the age-old story of the church re-adventuring into the world.

Wendell Belew tells of a church in Philadelphia that started from backyard Bible study fellowships that meet in the summertime. Not only were there classes at night for adults, but also in the daytime for children, as part of the Vacation Bible School promotion.

Most fellowships are conducted in the homes, but not all of them. Some are in prisons, some in factories, some in schools, some in nursing homes, and some in hospitals.

7] [Pulpit Renewal of the Word

Last Sunday a man walked down the aisle of a church and said, "I surrender to God's call to preach. I have tried everything else, this is the life for which I was made." It will happen again next Sunday and on all Sundays to come until the end of time. God's voice is loose in the world. He is making prophets for himself as he has been making them since the days of the Old Testament. He lights a fire in men that becomes a fierce heat for action.

All men who have been called to preach know the pressure of a message that must be delivered. Jeremiah said, "His word was in mine heart as a burning fire shut up in my bones, and I was weary with forebearing and I could not stay" (Jer. 20:9). His bones burned with the word of God, and it had to come out.

Sometimes the fire that the preachers feel they cannot clearly see, and they have difficulty finding the exact words to express it. Nevertheless it must be spoken. This is why true preaching is never well-polished logic or tricky syllogisms, and why sometimes it seems incoherent and impractical. A sermon is not argument but fire—fire which God has kindled in the preacher. It burns with incredible effect in the lives of those who are serious enough about living to stop and listen.

Paul said, "I was made a minister according to the gift of the grace of God given unto me by the effectual working of his power" (Eph. 3:7). He did not call his compulsion a fire but the effect was the same. He said it was a grace given and that by preaching he should "make all men see" (v. 9). He made clear the commanding nature of the call, "Woe is unto me, if I preach not the gospel" (1 Cor. 9:16).

The call to preach is often elusive yet persistent. If it is not present, no amount of thinking can bring it into being; if it is present, there is never a moment when it is not felt. One man feels it, another does not; one gives up everything for it, the other views such sacrifice as senseless waste; one man will spend hours describing it, the other will declare that it is a dream of the imagination. The "still small voice" speaking within is a terrible reality to those who hear it and becomes for them a call of thunder and fire from which they cannot escape, while to others to whom God does not speak the special call, there is only silence.

Preaching is always under attack. A teen-ager says, "My mother preaches to me all the time." An alcoholic husband shouts at his wife, "Don't preach to me." A prominent pastor resigns his pulpit and says, "Preaching is dead." A young man comes to the seminary and says, "I'll serve any way except by preaching." A psychologist claims, "Preaching is the least effective way of imparting a message." A politician lowers his voice in the midst of an address and says, "I did not mean to be preaching." All of this suggests that preaching has a bad reputation.

One has only to turn to the New Testament to see that preaching can be an effective means of communicating truth. Jesus himself was a preacher. His message was the kingdom of God, the good news of God's love, and the judgments of God. His pulpit was everywhere, and his audience was the poor and the rich, the slave and the free. He gave explicit preaching instructions to his disciples, "Go ye . . . and preach the gospel to every creature" (Mark 16:15). His mandate was clear and compelling. "Preach" means "to herald," shout the love of God to every creature, call it out as a word of hope to drowning men. Lift your voice above all other voices to make it heard. *"Go"* as he used it means "press on," never be still, seize every opportunity, be always at work.

Jesus did not see the sermon as an intellectual literary form, but as a structure for experience. The gospel is not to be shut up in an argument, but to be lived in action. Preaching is not debate, but proclamation. It is not a passive calling, but an active one. Preaching is not retrospective but prophetic. As James David Randolph has put it, "Preaching is fundamentally invitational rather than analytical . . . not the packaging of a project but the evocation of an event."

Go preach! Spring to action, seize every opportunity, make every confrontation a pulpit, every experience an occasion. "In season, out of season" (2 Tim. 4:2) as Paul put it. It was Karl Barth who said that the preacher must "proclaim to his fellowmen what God himself has to say to them, by explaining, in his own words, a passage from the Scripture which concerns them personally."

Preaching is an intensive active personal thing, and must be based on tension between two great realities, the reality of the Word of God and the reality of the practical experiences of both preacher and people. P. T. Forsyth said, "The cure for pulpit dullness is not brilliancy, as in literature. It is reality." Preaching then becomes involvement with people and their problems, an effort to bring the Word of God to bear on the realities of the present-day world. The need for it is not likely to soon die, nor will the feeling of the church for the importance of it die; nevertheless, preaching is in trouble as it has not been in trouble in modern times.

Why is preaching in trouble? Surely some of the fault lies with the pew, but not all of it; some lies also with the pulpit.

1. Some preaching is not deeply rooted in the Bible. It takes its text but not its content from the Bible. One inventory of sermons preached in a revival meeting showed only personal stories, many of them not relevant to the gospel. The evangelist was an entertainer masquerading as a preacher. Such preaching is froth producing at best frothy church members.

2. Some preaching buries itself in the Bible without eyes or ears for what is taking place in the contemporary world. It is done as if there were no newspaper headlines, no compelling fiction, no great drama, no deep sociological currents and no serious history in formation in the world today. This does not mean that preaching should become a recital of the week's current events, but that the sermon should be an audible tension between the Word of God and all that transpires in life around the preacher. Indeed, if the gospel is addressed to contemporary man, it must take into account his daily life situation. Edmund Steimle said, "The sermon which starts in the Bible and stays in the Bible is not Biblical." He meant that unless the sermon penetrates deeply the filth and abscess of the modern mind and heart, it fails utterly to do that for which the Bible exists.

3. Some preaching is obviously secondhanded. The preacher simply borrows his convictions and materials from other people. The man frantically searching for a text on Saturday night has not learned to live deeply and thoughtfully with the Word of God. If he ruthlessly borrows the material of others, it means that his message is a

shallow message of the head, not a deep one of the heart. Church members without even realizing that the man is a phony will turn him off.

4. Some preaching studiously supplies the facts but neglects the fire. One preacher said, "I build an outline and fill it with material. Then I study to find the little speck of fire. When I find it, I start all over again, and this is my sermon." The man preaches to standing room only. His neighbor labors late into the night on his sermons, but fails to find the burning connection between the truth and his own heart; both he and his people are in trouble.

There is hope because as history plainly shows, preaching has always been in trouble, and yet has victoriously overcome its trouble. Renewal of the pulpit is possible in our day, provided both people and preacher are willing to recognize it as God's pulpit, not theirs, and as speaking God's words, not the words of man.

The Renewal of the Pulpit

"After all it is *not* the best of all possible worlds." This is the cry of those who have lived through wars and depressions and who have seen the generation come and go. They know it is the best available at the moment, but strongly feel it could be better.

What's wrong? Most popular answers analyze only the symptoms and deal only with the external scaffolding of life, the crisis factors displayed in the latest newspaper headlines. They do not deal with the roots of the problem, the great universal needs of man that have not altered since Adam first set foot on the earth. These analysts advocate improving the highway system, making better airplanes, planning more campsites, building a few more houses, sending a new delegation to Congress—and assume in doing this that they have dealt with the vital issues of man. But have they?

The desperation of our times is often measured in headlines like these:

Filth in the Air Destroys the Oxygen We Breathe
Pollution of the Rivers Spoils the Water We Drink
5,000 Hydrogen Bombs Threaten All Human Life
Overpopulation Makes the World an Intolerable Ball
800,000 Drug Addicts Steal Billions

My point is not the unimportance of the newspaper headlines, which we all know are quite important. It is that these problems, so often merely symptomatic, are considered as if a long list of basic human needs did not exist. One can be sure that if a scrawny little boy is suspended yelling and kicking in midair on a seesaw, there is a big fat bully on the other end. If a crisis problem keeps turning up in public life, one should look to the other end of the seesaw. Almost always, no matter how trite the suspended problem, at the bottom end is deep human spiritual need, unattended and unfulfilled.

Such headlines are true enough and it is our Christian duty to keep these tragedies in mind as long as such conditions exist; yet the plain truth is, we must go much deeper and find out what is making wars and dope addicts, or that causes man to spoil his air and his rivers. Christians whose lives are rooted in the word of God know that the real problem is unmet spiritual need and unsatisfied soul hunger.

H. H. Farmer, a leading English preacher has analyzed modern basic spiritual needs as follows: (1) "A certain underlying, depressed, hollow sense of the futility and meaninglessness of human existence." (2) Individuals today are "oppressed by a sense of their personal insignificance." (3) "A yearning for security." (4) "A rather shocked, and even frightened awareness of the power of what can only be called the forces of evil and of unreason which is at work in the world today." (5) "A feeling of need for an absolute in conduct." [1] These personal losses hang like ghosts in the hearts of many men; pastors emerging from their counseling rooms will tell you that they are at the bottom of many personal distresses. They show the pathetic lostness of modern man.

"The Futility and Meaninglessness of Human Existence"

One cannot go into the great ghettos of New York City without being appalled at the masses of disoriented people living so close together with so much hatred. Signs of it are everywhere: crude obscenities scrawled on the walls, broken windows, filth, fights, theft, muggings, drunkenness, and sexual assault. Anger overflows into the whole city and suddenly it is believed by some to be the unsafest and dirtiest place on earth. Thousands of subway cars bear the same obscenities written with spray paint, inside and out. "Graffiti" these markings are called, after the ancient cave writings of the Romans, but the real name is the desperation that rises from human meaninglessness.

Graffiti are written by youth without causes, human souls without sense of meaning and awareness of destiny. Many of those who write are without jobs and fit places to live, the social scientists say, and there is truth in this; yet one feels that this is only a surface explanation. The real cause of human meaninglessness is too much social dislocation too quick, too much emphasis on the standards of materialism, and an erosion of personal awareness of human accountability to Almighty God.

The hippies that have roamed the country, the aimlessness of youth who do not see life as opportunity or stewardship, the surrender of a whole generation to sexual promiscuity, the search of youth for the ultimate physical experience whatever it is, are signs of this universal emptiness. We've always had such people, "Clouds they are without water, carried about of winds; trees whose fruit withereth, without fruit, twice dead, plucked up by the roots; raging waves of the sea, foaming out their own shame; wandering stars" (Jude 12-13).

Some shave their heads and put on the pastel robes of the Buddhists, others enter the dark and cruel world of drugs, and others follow the false prophets of Christianity into orgies of drunkenness and fornication. The manna they eat is far from satisfying, as most of them are quick to say. It does not go to the marrow, but becomes just one more tough binding shell around their hollow souls.

At the bottom of all personal futility and meaninglessness is the sin of no faith. It is a sign of the lostness of the human soul, of its alienation from God. Such people are "without God and without hope," to use Paul's words.

Mere human words cannot reach them. Only the word of God powerfully and persistently presented can crack all of those hard human shells. There are at least a thousand texts for dealing with their emptiness and meaninglessness. For the people who hunger for cosmic significance there is Romans 8:28: "We know that all things work together for good to them that love God, to them who are the called according to his purpose." And Ephesians 3:9, "Make all men see what is the fellowship of the mystery, which from the beginning of the world hath been hid in God, who created all things by Jesus

Christ."

For those who want a sense of true greening in a spiritual desert there is Psalm 1:1–3: "Blessed is the man . . . [whose] delight is in the law of the Lord; and in his law doth he meditate day and night. And he shall be like a tree planted by the rivers of water, that bringeth forth his fruit in his season; his leaf also shall not wither; and whatsoever he doeth shall prosper." The availability of such texts with which to confront hoards of tough hollow men are as good arguments for the need for preaching as any that ever existed. No weak or timid preachers need apply, for preaching these texts is a job for men of steel who from bended knees speak the whole counsel of God.

Personal Insignificance

The loss of healthy ego is one of the universal sicknesses of our times. The tragedy is that so many of its worst victims never admit it. Inside they are cringing pygmies, while outside they pretend to be strong and self-sufficient. Stubborn and wilful, proud and defiant, and even aggressive and overbearing, their sickness is still there making them feel cowed and insufficient.

Jesus knew their sickness, and could pierce it with a single question, as when he dealt with the woman at the well driving a bold shaft straight into her pride by asking, "Woman where is thy husband?" He knew that her problem was guilt, which is precisely what it is with so many people who feel personally insignificant today. He offered forgiveness of sins, for he knew that the more guilt she carried the less likely she was able to function as valid and whole individual.

Some modern psychologists accuse Christianity of fostering guilt, but Christians who know the New Testament know that they are wrong. Christianity fosters the elimination of guilt through the forgiveness of sin. Jesus offers abounding freedom, "I am come that they might have life, and that they might have it more abundantly" (John 10:10). He does not offer indiscriminate forgiveness, but only forgiveness in response to repentance. Some psychologists do not recognize any kind of sin, and therefore do not recognize any kind of guilt, even unrepented guilt. When Jesus said to the lame man in the pool of Siloam who had been defeated again and again, "Rise, take up your bed and walk," he was striking at his lameness, his sin and his shattered ego. Jesus wanted the poor fellow to quit wallowing in the mud and stand up and be a man, but the man could not respond until he was willing to turn his back on his sin.

The incredible sensitiveness one encounters today in such things as defensiveness, touchiness, tension, alibiing, anger, resentment, envy, and even open paranoia are certain signs of all kinds of hidden guilt for which Jesus offers ego-enhancing forgiveness. This points to the human condition of lostness. To feel insignificant is to be without friends, and that is exactly the predicament of the lost soul. It is not the friend of God, and lacking this friendship it is sick, desperately sick, seeing itself as the center of its own little universe, and carrying with it always the vision of wayward and unredeemed self-image.

The Bible has a message for the sick guilty ego. It begins with God's great concern for the first man, "Adam, you are important, you've got a name and I have spoken it. Give the animals their names, give the woman her name. Replenish the earth, subdue the earth. Adam stand up." God said also, "Cain, you are responsible, you are indeed your brother's keeper." He said to Moses, "Moses, Moses, you are my leader, deliver my people." "The Lord is love unfailing, and great is his power to set men free" (Ps. 130:7, NEB).

Let the preachers preach God's indwelling presence through Christ to all men of doubtful spirit and weak hearts. "Do you not understand that Christ is Jesus within you? Otherwise you must be failures" (2 Cor. 13:5, Moffatt). This is not a job for a cringing apologetic preacher, who refuses to take the Scriptures directly into every condition of human life. A wise aggressive use of the Word of God is "sharper than any two-edged sword," will restore self-respect and self-esteem to many a cowed and defeated sinner.

"Yearning for Security"

Farmer stressed two kinds of insecurity. One he called relative insecurity and compared it with the bursting of water pipes, the other he called radical and fundamental insecurity and compared it with an earthquake. Most people are concerned about water pipe security; yet when things get tough the water pipes seem only as straws, and they cry out for a deeper kind of security more related to the meaning of life than the comfort of life. When life goes to pieces, they want the security that comes from an orderly understanding of the universe and of the human situation.

Once while I was sitting with missionary friends in an eighth-floor Tokyo department store restaurant, the whole building began to move with an awesome rumbling noise. It was an earthquake, no doubt about it. Dishes rattled, lights swung like pendulums, waiters dropped to their knees, children cried, people quit talking and one of the missionaries said, "I've been here twenty-six years and this is the worst." To steady myself I put my hand on a huge concrete pillar, only to find it shaking too. There was no security anywhere for the foundations of the whole earth were shaking.

Modern man lives in a constant earthquake and goes from one quivering pillar to another. His whole social and economic world is changing and he wants security which he finds nowhere; there is no solid ground anymore, so it seems to disconsolate and frightened man. David the king knew this feeling when Absalom organized his rag-tag army and laid seige on the palace. He cried out, "Lift me up and set me up on a rock, for thou hast been my shelter, a tower for refuge from the enemy" (Ps. 61:2–3, NEB). Here again is a sign of the lost soul, the man without any kind of moral and spiritual grounding, either temporal or eternal.

The Bible is full of texts to reassure the weak and the afraid who are looking for a strong pillar to lean against and a solid rock to stand on. Jesus said, " 'I am the light of the world, no follower of mine shall wander in the dark' " (John 8:12, NEB); and " 'I am the bread of life. Whoever comes to me shall never be hungry' " (John 6:35, NEB). God's word speaks strong words to man's need for security, more strongly than Jesus' promise. " 'The man who comes to me I will never turn away' " (John 6:37, NEB).

"The Forces of Evil and Unreason Which Are at Work in History"

The historians have a long argument going, some say God breaks into history; some say he does not. Believers like Arnold Toynbee and Kenneth Latourette hold that the long stream of history shows God entering again and again into the great events of history to correct the excesses and depravities of man, and to shape history toward a redemptive end. Skeptics like Thomas Carlyle and H. G. Wells said that history is no more than the folly of man unfolding itself, and that God is never in any sense a factor of history.

Both groups, however, would quickly admit that there is a deep undercurrent force of evil and unreason that works throughout all human kind. Floods of evil lead to crime, blundering economics to national debt, arms buildup to bloody wars, and the wisest of men seem powerless to do anything about them. The drift alarms and frightens us, and we pray for some way to beat it. Without God in our lives, the whole maze of history becomes an endless and senseless jungle. We are lost with the feeling that the world is piling in on top of us, and that we have no place to hide.

Evil forces cannot work in the masses without working in individuals. They pervade the hearts of men, taking away their innocence, twisting their motives and turning them into monsters. Paul described the results: "Dead in trespasses and sins; wherein in times past ye walked according to the course of this world, according to the prince of the power of the air, the spirit that now worketh in the children of disobedience" (Eph. 2:1-2). Sin lies at the door of every human soul, and as it shapes men, it shapes history. Dealing with the forces of evil and unreason at work in history is one of the fundamental challenges to the preacher. People want answers. Why evil? Why unreason? What can be done about it? Only men with fire in their bones like Jeremiah and whose lips have been touched by the coal off the altar like Isaiah (Isa. 6:6-7) can answer questions like these.

"An Absolute for Conduct"

Man can live only so long out of a suitcase. The time comes when he needs the same bed every night, the same familiar street every morning, the same friends every day. Travel is fine for short periods of time, but as an endless thing, it will drive the strongest man up the wall. Man was built for fixed landmarks, and must have them if he is going to contribute meaningfully to society.

Man's moral and spiritual world must also have some fixed landmarks. It is important for him that the sun always rise, and that it rise today about where it rose yesterday. The standards by which he fixes his values must not change if he is to function with a whole heart and an integrated mind. Without the Magna Charta England would have fallen long ago, and without the Constitution and the Bill of Rights America would not have survived even her first few years of life. Some absolutes are necessary for human fitness and productivity.

Strange minds have joined to attack all absolutes. They argue that nothing is wrong and nothing is right, and that there is no fixed value of any kind; all ethics are relative, all laws are arbitrary, all realities are dissolute, and all judgments are capricious. The most glaring of these new philosophies are that God is dead and all his law with him, and that right and wrong are merely a manner of speaking. The theology of Thomas J. Altizer who advanced the idea that God is dead and the morality of Hugh Hefner who created the "playboy" philosophy threaten the moral and spiritual equilibrium of man. One takes away the leg of faith and the other the leg of sincerity, and the legless torso of humanity rolls with the winds into oblivion. The deep-seated cry of the whole human race is against this, for most men demand absolutes. They want to know what is fixed and what is not fixed, what is right and what is not right. They want something concrete by which to live. They want their preachers to be prophets and to speak with conviction the whole counsel of God.

Can you imagine your confusion if suddenly the north star began to wobble in its orbit as the magnetic compass began to point in different directions? Well, this is precisely what is happening today with moral and spiritual values. They are not really changing, but men think they are changing, and this is bringing deep inward personal chaos. There is no other word except "lost" to describe man's denial of absolutes.

Preachers must say to the whole world, "This I believe . . . here I stand." The crucial texts are more meaningful than ever, such texts as "Heaven and earth shall pass away: but my words shall not pass away" (Luke 21:33); and "Jesus Christ the same yesterday, and today, and for ever" (Heb. 13:8). The ancient precepts, most notably the Ten Commandments, are still the law of God, and stand reverseless and indeclinable as God's spiritual and moral word for today. These are not the ten suggestions of God, but the ten laws of God. No preacher need apologize for preaching them as laws, for they are as fresh and relevant as the latest statute passed by Congress and signed by the President. In fact, they are more relevant, because they deal with the vital nature of man, and speak to his need for absolutes.

The Quickening of the Preacher

When did modern events camouflage preaching as the central

event of the Anglo-Saxon community? Was it with the coming of the public school? The advent of scientism? Or was it the rise of pluralism? Who can say? The factors are many and complex.

One view is that it started when the phrase "on the other hand" was introduced into the pulpit. No one would take this view seriously, yet there is something to be said for it. Paul warned, "Though I speak with the tongues of men and of angels, and have not charity, I am become as sounding brass, or a tinkling cymbal" (1 Cor. 13:1) and "If the trumpet give an uncertain sound, who shall prepare himself to the battle?" (1 Cor. 14:8). One who would preach must believe what he preaches.

He can camouflage his doubts for a time, and fool some of the people; yet he cannot fool himself or God, and in the end he will fool none. There is no room for tinkling cymbals and uncertain trumpets in the pulpit.

P. T. Forsyth said, "With its preaching Christianity stands or falls." The critic may say that this is an extreme claim for the oratory, but Forsyth did not say "oratory" he said "preaching," and in his mind there is a difference. "The Christian preacher is not the successor of the Greek orator, but of the Hebrew prophet. The orator comes with but an inspiration, the prophet comes with a revelation." Oratory plays the galleries, preaching minds the gospel; oratory takes passing fancy as its subject, preaching draws from the Word of God; oratory calls for marching, preaching for redemption. Forsyth continues: "The orator, at most, may urge men to love their brother, the preacher beseeches them to be reconciled to their Father. With preaching Christianity stands or falls because it is the declaration of a gospel. Nay more—far more—*it is the gospel prolonging and declaring itself.*"[2]

"The Gospel Prolonging and Declaring Itself"

Preaching is not a profession but a calling. It is not a choice of jobs, but a surrender to a cause. When Paul said, "I am apprehended of Christ Jesus" (Phil. 3:12), he was no doubt speaking of himself as a preacher as well as a Christian. Against his will he became a Christian, and in the face of savage enemies he became a preacher. Jesus Christ seized him and changed his ambition. This is the basis of all effective preaching, broken worldly ambitions and captured by Jesus.

Preaching is more than words, more than speeches and more than stated hours of worship. It is all this, but unless it becomes a part of the movement of the Spirit of God into the hearts of men, it is empty rhetoric, and not worth its time and effort. Preaching is like recruiting of the army or navy, the object is not to make beautiful speeches or to go through routines, but to enlist the man. The recruiter is the army prolonging and declaring itself, the preacher is the gospel prolonging and declaring itself. Recruitment seeks the enlistee, preaching seeks the decider. Enlistees merely join the army or navy, new Christians become the kingdom of God. The gospel is everlastingly evangelistic, which means that true preaching, whatever its form, must also be invitational, having the purposes of convicting, converting, and conserving. The preacher who says, "Woe is me if I preach not the gospel," feels the living thrust of Christ searching, seeking, prolonging, and declaring himself. He must speak as part of a river of living water that flows from Calvary.

Freshness in preaching is not the presence of glittering new illustrations. These may help bridge the chasm between the minds of the preacher and the unbelievers, but they are never a substitute for experience. True freshness in preaching is a new experience with the gospel. Touched by the Spirit of Christ and endued with a new insight into the old truth, the preacher is fired with living power, and behind him is the life of God, and the words he speaks are spoken by God. He stands in the pulpit with a certain trumpet. In fact, he is the trumpet, and God is the breath of the trumpet, and the sound of the trumpet is the voice of God.

The Preacher's Thought Is Not His Own

"He does not create truth; he bears witness to the truth," wrote Donald G. Miller. "Whatever freshness he has is not the freshness of novelty, but the freshness of insight into what the church has always believed. He does not initiate new truth, but appropriates old truth. His spontaneity is not to be the discovery of that which others never knew, but rather the 'spontaneity of power' in appropriating and enforcing the revelation made by God in Christ—a revelation already full, final, and complete, always believed by the church universal. It's not the minister's place to say a new thing, but *to say an old thing with new power.*"[3]

"To Say an Old Thing with New Power"

The preacher's source book is the Bible, not only for the message he preaches but also for the strengthening of his own life. It is his own special oracle, his preacher that speaks to him the message of God. Until he sees it as supremely binding in his own life, he has no way of making it come alive in the lives of others. Until it becomes daily experience his preaching will be as thin as water and as elusive as the white space between the lines of this sentence.

The primary content of the sermon is not the mere words of the Scripture, but the words in tension with the preacher. "The book is a cold lifeless record until the Spirit guides us to the presence of the living Christ, who awaits us within, at the very center of the book," is the way Harold Tribble said it. "Once we have followed the Spirit to find God in his word we will earnestly seek to have him lead us on that we may increasingly know God." The Bible is an ancient book, one of the oldest in the world. The preacher's obligation is to the old book; yet he must always be preaching it with new power, his own special power given to him by the Holy Spirit as he meets Christ in its pages.

"No sermon is a preacher's free creation," said Theodore A. Gill. "The communication he will point to in his address is God's very own. The whole point of all the preacher's saying will be what God has already said." God is the beginner and finisher of all sermons; the preacher's part is simply to be the Spirit-filled catalyst of the moment.

Preachers who draw on the Bible for their text never lack preaching material. Spurgeon who preached the Bible did not repeat himself in thirty-five hundred printed sermons. He said, "After thirty-five years, I find the quarry of Holy Scripture inexhaustible, I seem hardly to have begun to labor in it." Compare this to topical preachers you have known who repeat themselves every six months. The Scriptures are like a vast unexplored continent, the broad rivers and high mountains we know, but the caves and the creeks are scarcely known to us at all, and in them we find the diamonds and the gold.

Preaching then is exploration, or rather the account of exploration, but different from ordinary geographical exploration, it becomes a living transformation of spiritual discovery into the lives of the hearers. It is not mere discovery of places and things, but discovery of a Person, and the introduction of that Person to those who hear. It is the discovery of Christ and then introducing him to the people. There is an "indissoluble oneness of preaching and the Christian faith," said H. H. Farmer.

This "indissoluble oneness" makes the preacher far more than an orator, because his involvement in the message makes him part of the message. Forsyth said that preaching of the cross "is part of the action of the Cross." The word of the cross "is really the Cross's own energy, the Cross in action. . . . *The real presence of Christ is what makes preaching.* It is what makes of a speech a sermon, and of a sermon Gospel."

"The Real Presence of Christ Is What Makes Preaching"

Preaching is not moralizing or character building; it is not lesson making or value building. This does not mean that it ignores morals, character, lessons, and values, but that they are all by-products of preaching. They come as incidental to the steel framework that is the heart of the gospel. The failure of much preaching is due to its preoccupation with morals and values to the point of excluding the cross which takes all life out of law and puts it under grace.

Preaching is primarily the proclamation of a person who came to us in an event. It is the celebration of the advent of Christ into the world. Peter in a one-man sermon to Cornelius spoke of God "preaching [good news of] peace by Christ Jesus" (Acts 10:36). He then spoke of the death and resurrection of Christ.

The primary credentials of the preacher is that he is a Christian and that he preaches Christ. If he is merely a moralizer, he will be laughed at and despised, and the temptation of all preachers is to take the easy way of moralizing. Much of the criticism against preaching today is due to its loss of its theological backbone and that it does not convincingly announce the presence of Christ in the world.

The Bible is a solid and infallible source of truth about God. Its presence in the world is both miracle and mystery, but as great as the Bible is, our final appeal is not to the Bible but to the gospel. The event of Christ in the world is the reality which gives the Bible its meaning. A sinner may deny the Bible, but in the end he cannot deny the gospel. It is the gospel that leads him to accept the Bible, not the Bible that leads him to accept the gospel. At the bottom of all authentic preaching is the real presence of Christ. It is the historical and eminent Christ announcing himself to the world through the preacher. Preaching is Christ prolonging and declaring himself.

The quickening of the preacher will come as he sees himself totally involved in his message. His preaching is not something that he does but is something that he is. He expresses himself not merely to fulfil a professional commitment, but to advance a cause. In proportion to his depth of involvement in his message, will be his success. "True preaching," Donald Miller said, "is not achieved until the words of the preacher becomes the Deed of God." The preacher succeeds because he is part of the Deed himself.

His quickening is also related to his willingness to "preach for a verdict," as our fathers used to say. Preaching that is not forward looking toward securing commitment is sterile and the product of a sterile heart. The quickened preacher always moves toward decision. Jesus said, "Behold I stand at the door *and knock.*" Preaching is a partnership in knocking on the doors of the hearts of men. It is calling for attention, a summons to the will, a friend beckoning, a brother bearing good news. The quickened preacher will feel himself in the midst of supreme action, as involved in the works of God when he stands to preach, only if he senses his partnership with God in capturing the souls of men.

Renewal will come to any preacher who (1) understands preaching to be the gospel at work through him prolonging and declaring itself, (2) sees his message as the ancient word of God clothed in new power, (3) surrenders to the real presence of Christ as the power of his sermon, (4) dedicates himself to preaching for a verdict every time he stands to preach, (5) preaches only what he experiences and believes.

The Rebuilding of the Pulpit

The American pulpit no longer holds the admiring respect of the general public. Its enemies are often slanderous, and its friends counter-vailing. The enemies cry "sham" and "pretense," and the friends are personally critical of the preacher. Modern novelists picture the pulpit as weak, selfish, and parasitical; and modern church members picture it as irrelevant, insincere, and commercial. Both are doing irreparable damage to the influence of the gospel in the modern world.

The reasons given for this attack on the pulpit reflect a total misunderstanding of its place and purpose. The enemies say that the pulpit (1) preaches an archaic and meaningless religion, (2) self-dramatizes itself as a moral and spiritual hero, (3) fails to deal constructively with the real human issues of the time, (4) preys upon the emotional ignorance of the people, (5) claims as fact some ideas completely unsupported by evidence, and (6) presents secondhanded experiences clothed in plagiarized words. Obviously, such generalizations are totally wrong and totally inept. Yet all kinds of people accept them as facts and stereotype the pulpit after their painful and inadequate image.

The counter-vailing friends are not much better. They say (1) the pulpit is irrelevant and ineffectual, (2) the preachers have forgotten their spiritual motivation, (3) the sermons are dull and inconsequential, (4) the preachers stay too much with the Bible or they desert the Bible altogether, (5) sermons are secondhanded and unrehearsed, (6) preachers do not give enough attention to modern communications techniques, (7) preaching is too much above the heads of the people, (8) preaching does not touch where they live. Most of us would agree that there is some truth in these criticisms; yet would deny that any of them prevail universally.

The real reasons for the decline of prestige are much deeper. The outright enemy of preaching (1) cannot stand the moral demands of the gospel, (2) cannot accept the searchlight of the Holy Spirit as his own life, (3) is trapped by scientism and refuses faith as one of the great motivations of life, (4) will not accept the discipline of the fellowship of the gospel, and (5) has himself surrendered the spirit of this age to the power of the air.

The counter-vailing church member has (1) failed to make a total commitment, (2) has not learned to make allowances and exceptions, (3) does not see himself responsible for the ministry and mission of the church, (4) has not caught the true meaning of the gospel, (5) has not seen his role as auxiliary to the minister. There is some truth here, yet they are generalizations that cannot apply to all situations.

At the bottom of all criticism of the pulpit is sin, and where the pulpit is indeed weak, there also is sin. It may be that the sin of the pulpit is failure to make clear the judgments of God against sin, and that the rebuilding of the pulpit must start with the preacher's willingness to face up to his responsibilty as a prophet of God. The preacher for the new times of moral reprobation and ethical apostasy must see the words of God as having everlasting freshness in their ability to dissect and destroy the cancerous impurities of the human soul. Yet the true preacher who really wants to rebuild his pulpit will hold himself in balance by declaring the whole counsel of God. He will not piecemeal or hyphenate the Bible, but present it wholly, withholding nothing.

Donald G. Miller suggests a threefold function of the Bible: (1) To reveal God, the living God; (2) to reveal man to himself in the light of God; and (3) to announce the 'good news' that the estranged relationship between them is to be overcome by the costly redemptive action of a loving God, and that man should live in the power of this redemption." Rebuilding the pulpit depends on both preacher and people seeing these functions as the primary responsibilities of the pulpit.

"To Reveal God, the Living God"

The pulpit that sees itself as responsible for setting forth God in a clear light will feel a new vitality and a new sense of presence with the audience. When John said of Jesus, "The word was made flesh . . . and we beheld his glory" (John 1:14), he was focusing on Christ as the revealer, the living God. It was an exciting moment for John as if he were saying, "At last, at long last, we see God, the living God."

The preacher that takes the pulpit seriously will see himself standing there in Christ's stead, speaking as the mouthpiece of God. For the moment he is the message made flesh. If he truly presents God, he is not merely officiating at a podium or presiding at a meeting, he is fighting in the arena of light and reality. He is the living voice through whom God is speaking. Men will listen, because they cannot help but listen. Like an electric arc on a dark dreary day, the pulpit will burn, for it is indeed the living vortex where the currents strike to form the fire.

Men will look because in the gloom there is no other light so bright and no other fire so warm. God will honor any place where men speak of him as supreme, as alive, and as present. The preacher's ability to do this depends on how well he knows the Bible and how much he immerses himself in its message. He cannot truly speak of God except in biblical terms, for this is how God reveals himself. If he speaks the true voice of God he must speak out of the Bible.

"To Reveal Man to Himself, in the Light of God"

The serious pulpit speaks from God to man about God and about man. It uses the Bible to unlock for man the mystery of his humanity and his divinity. If it deals in mere trivialities and moralities, it cheapens itself and drives men away, but if it meaningfully explains man to himself, so that man sees himself as in a mirror, then the pulpit will take on new dignity and will attract men. The best tool the preacher has for this kind of analysis is the Bible.

This suggests what Howard T. Kuist of Princeton Seminary has called the *instrumental* value of the Scripture. The Bible is the scalpel for dissecting the sins of man, the pen for writing indelible convictions on the human heart, and the mirror in which man sees himself as lost and undone, the word which commands the most defiant and cynical ear, the schoolmaster that teaches him the law and the ladder that provides a way out of his despair. If the pulpit makes clear the word of God, it becomes God speaking in a way which the hearer cannot mistake for the voice of any other. It does not require pragmatic proof, but is its own proof as men bear against their choices and are converted against their wills.

". . . the Costly Redemptive Action of a Loving God

The only justification for the existence of any pulpit is Jesus Christ, but not Jesus Christ as uninvolved in the lives and affairs of men. Too much of today's preaching about Christ is transcendent, as if it belonged on the ceiling and not in the heart of men. It is so distant and so unreal that men turn away puzzled, the pulpit having failed to bring it out of history and out of the air into the reality of the human experience. If the pulpit is to rebuild itself in modern times, Jesus

Christ must be made real to the consciousnesses and to consciences of men.

The pulpit is indeed the announcer of God's love and sacrifice. It makes clear that God and man are not on friendly terms, and that God has taken the essential step toward reconciliation. No matter where the pulpit goes in the Bible in search of its message, it is always returning to the central idea of the Bible, that God emptied himself through Christ into the lives of men, that on the cross the price for friendship was paid with the death of Christ, and that the hope for friendship was sealed with the resurrection of Christ. No other book in the world has this message except the Bible, and its meaning and significance is written on almost every page. No other verse sums it up like Romans 5:8: "God commendeth his love toward us, in that, while we were yet sinners, Christ died for us."

"Man Should Live in the Power of This Redemption"

If anything characterizes this generation more than others, it is that in spite of all his material prosperity, man has not learned the secret of triumphant living. The feverish search for new companions in sex, new highs in drugs, new causes to protest, new sins to exploit are blazing billboards advertising man's spiritual and emotional inadequacy. The abundant life is sought by everyone, but found by few. The seekers have not known where to look.

The verile pulpit knows the secret of abundant life and can tell the seekers where to find it—the Bible for it is an open manual of abundant living, and the power of that living is the death and resurrection of Jesus Christ. The truly adequate defenders of the pulpit know how to speak about his power because they have lived it. They can say with Paul, "I can do all things through Christ which strengtheneth me" (Phil. 4:13). When the preacher is alive to the daily needs of his people for sheer spiritual and emotional survival, the pulpit becomes a magnet of abiding power and a lamp of white compelling light.

An empty pulpit means an empty church. If there is compassion and power behind the sacred desk, then there will be no open hearts and minds in the pews. For the serious preacher, "Feed my sheep," becomes a personal call to teach the people to live by the words of Christ. He knows that this is what builds the pulpit.

Share the Word now, and rebuild the pulpit. Follow these simple steps to the strongest pulpit of your life: (1) Use the Scriptures to teach God's living presence, (2) use the Scriptures to show man to himself, (3) use the Scriptures to show man how God reaches out for him, (4) use the Scriptures to tell man how to live in the power of Christ.

Notes

Chapter Two

  [1] Clyde Reid, *The God-Evaders* (New York: Harper, 1966), p. 19.
  [2] Elton Trueblood, *Your Other Vocation* (New York: Harper, 1952), pp. 30–31.
  [3] F. Dean Lueking, *The Future of the Christian World Mission* (St. Louis: Concordia, 1971).
  [4] Harvey Cox, *God's Revolution and Man's Responsibility* (Valley Forge: Judson Press, 1965), p. 29.

Chapter Three

  [1] *The American Bible Society Record,* December, 1971, p. 185.
  [2] Rice A. Pierce, *Leading Dynamic Bible Study* (Nashville: Broadman Press, 1969), pp. 28–29.

Chapter Four

  [1] A. M. Chirgwin, *The Bible in World Evangelism* (New York: Association Press, 1954), p. 78; italics added.
  [2] Samuel Shoemaker, *By the Power of God* (New York: Harper, 1954), pp. 27–28.
  [3] Elton Trueblood, *The Company of the Committed* (New York: Harper, 1961), pp. 44–45.

Chapter Five

  [1] Roland Allen, *Missionary Methods: St. Paul's and Ours* (Grand Rapids: Eerdmans, 1962), p. 23.
  [2] D. T. Niles, *The Message and the Messenger* (Nashville: Abingdon, 1966), p. 41.

Chapter Six

  [1] Robert W. Lynn and Elliot Wright, *The Big Little School* (New York: Harper, 1971), p. xl.
  [2] Howard Grimes, *The Rebirth of the Laity* (Nashville: Abingdon, 1962), p. 193.
  [3] John L. Casteel, *Spiritual Renewal Through Personal Groups* (New York: Association, 1957), pp. 212–13.
  [4] Bill Glass, *Get in the Game!* (Waco: Word, 1965), pp. 47–48.
  [5] David J. Ernsberger, *Reviving the Local Church* (Philadelphia: Fortress, 1969), p. 75.

Chapter Seven

  [1] H. H. Farmer, *The Servant of the Word* (Philadelphia: Fortress, 1942), p. 96.
  [2] P. T. Forsythe, *Positive Preaching and the Modern Mind* (Grand Rapids: Eerdmans, 1967), pp. 1–3.
  [3] Donald G. Miller, *Fire in Thy Mouth* (Nashville: Abingdon Press, 1954), p. 110.